Entertaining

MICK and NICK NOSH started their business collaboration in 1992, becoming renowned for their celebrity parties, after both had enjoyed extensive careers in the media, music and entertainment industries, and apprenticeships in kitchens around the world. Unable to find a restaurant in London to serve them the type of food they wanted to eat, in the surroundings in which they wanted to eat, the food served as they wanted it to be served, they opened their own in London's Fulham Road in 1993. Their reputation for great entertaining and superb, honest 'food with attitude' rapidly grew, and won wide critical acclaim. Following on from their recent Talk Radio food and drink programme and many other magazine, television and radio appearances, their barbecuing TV series, *Red Hot & Smokin'*, has appeared on the Carlton Food Network, soon to be followed by *Winter Nosh*.

THE
NOSH BROTHERS

PHOTOGRAPHS BY KELVIN MURRAY

MACMILLAN

Acknowledgements

We are grateful to the following for inspiration and assistance:

Bente Stein, the Mothers Nosh, Gill Best, Marie Hekimian, Tony McIntosh, Chris Quayle, Kelvin Murray, Anthony Critchlow, Vanessa Biddulph, Dilly Godfrey-Wild, Simon Hopkinson, Dan Schickentanz, the Meat and Livestock Commission, Rayners, David Mellor, Susan Fleming, John Sachs, Anthony Blackburn, Bruce Warwick, George Allans, Juliet Alexander, Oliver Maude-Roxby.

First published 1997 by Macmillan

an imprint of Macmillan Publishers Ltd
25 Eccleston Place, London SW1W 9NF
and Basingstoke

Associated companies throughout the world

ISBN 0 333 71608 6

1 3 5 7 9 8 6 4 2

A CIP catalogue record for this book is available from the British Library.

Designed by Macmillan General Books Design Department

Typeset by Florencetype Ltd, Stoodleigh, Devon
and Macmillan General Books Design Department

Photographic reproduction by Speedscan Ltd, Basildon, Essex

Printed and bound in Italy by Manfrini

Contents

Introduction 7

The Nosh Guide to Cooking and Entertaining 8

Menus for the Poor
17

Menus for the Well Off
53

Menus for the Rich
105

Accompaniments 141

Index 157

Introduction

By now you may have browsed through a great number of cookbooks ranging from simple stage-by-stage 'how-to' books – that are purely instructional – to glossy, inspirational coffee-table tomes. We hope this Nosh Brothers cookbook inspires you to improve your range of creative ideas and boosts your confidence to cook for occasions from a casual supper for friends to a birthday or other important anniversary.

You should not be nervous about tackling any new ideas here as recipes are presented in an easy-to-read format that talks you through the preparation and cooking process as if we were advising you in person. You won't find any dictatorial 'bullet points', but detailed, easy-to-follow reminders and tips on how to get the best results. All our ideas are achievable at home with a degree of effort that varies from easy to moderate. Our philosophy is that few things in the world of cuisine are actually difficult – mostly, it is a matter of careful preparation, patience and practice.

In addition, we have followed our own preferences in removing any complicated jargon or need for a professional level of equipment, the accent being on maximizing taste with easy access to ingredients (with a few exceptions) and using kitchen tools found at any good supermarket. Our aim in writing the Nosh Brothers' book has been to produce a light-hearted, amusing guide to entertaining as a whole. It is not intended to be used as a rigid or old-fashioned guide to etiquette. You will often find us irreverent with (we hope) an unpretentious style, that dispenses with the delicate food rules of the 1980s and the politically correct diktats of the Health and Taste Police.

To help you find out which menu suits you best, we have divided them into three main categories: for the poor (low budget); for the well off (medium budget); and for the rich (these contain ingredients that can be expensive). Of course, even if normally your budget is restricted, it doesn't prevent you from going 'up-market' for that special occasion. Also, you can use your common sense to substitute cheaper alternatives that work just as well.

At the beginning of some recipes you'll find illustrative icons that will give a quick easy guide to the type of recipe it is, such as whether it's a vegetarian dish, if it has rich ingredients, if care is needed or if you can pre-prepare the meal.

All recipes are proven, functional and deliver excellent results with their foolproof methods and advice. They are all written to be in correct proportions for eight people, with good appetites, so if you've four guests, cut the quantities in half. (But use your common sense to adjust the cooking times accordingly.)

This doesn't mean that if you have a degree of flair as a cook you can't invent your own additions and flourishes. Indeed, that's how cooking evolves – someone has a good idea, another takes it and improves it. Others call it stealing, but we reckon it's really evolution . . .

The Nosh Guide to Cooking and Entertaining

Ever since man first invited his neighbours over from the next cave to share a piece of mammoth, food has been the focus of a communal activity that nourishes both the body and soul. The ritual of entertaining always involves food and drink, and is the medium by which people can measure their status and identify and bond with each other. In some cases, keeping up with the Joneses becomes the main reason for reciprocal entertaining. Sometimes, it's just about getting over-refreshed with a few mates.

Planning the Party

Creating a successful event involves some degree of chemistry:

- a good mix of guests
- a suitable choice of food
- drink that complements the food
- the 'right' atmosphere.

One can't buy atmosphere but here are a few guidelines to getting it right.

The Guest List

Choose reliable guests (not people who have a reputation for turning up late or not showing up at all).

Make a list of your potential guests, dividing them in to A, B or C lists, according to their sociability. This is an important exercise, and you can use this for many occasions – not just a dinner party. You can mix certain groups, say A with B, but be careful, not too many Bs with As, otherwise the A friends will think you only know Bs.

A word of warning – never mix any Cs with As. This is bound to cause trouble.

A list – Top friends, always fun, reliable, bring plenty of good wine, will talk to anybody, offer to help with the clearing-up, and will send a note or phone their thanks for the event.

B list – You must downgrade your friends to a lower status if, for example, they have suspect table manners – like eating with their mouth open, talking with their mouth full or holding their knife as if it were a writing implement – and/or don't necessarily mix easily with other guests. Particular candidates for this group are people with eating disorders, e.g. vegetarians (and worse still, vegans), allergy wimps and people with strange beliefs and religious restrictions about diet. Not forgetting clumsy people who trash your home, by spilling wine or food on your carpet, etc.

C list – These people are generally a bit scuzzy, have little manners and unsophisticated palates in that they eat only beans on toast, fish fingers or pizza. If you yourself fit into this category please take this book back to the shop where you bought it with the receipt and get a refund, as it will be of little use to you.

If it is a sit-down meal, work out the number of people you can comfortably sit down around the table.

If you have a limited number of sit-down places and you want more people than you can sit, then you'll all just have to stand.

Always choose people you like. As a rule, people you dislike make dreadful guests.

The Menu

First, check your bank balance – this will guide you to the menu you can eat. First Direct (amongst many others) are great – you can check your balance by phone.

If you find that you have too many vegetarian friends, or are a vegetarian yourself, stop now. You have little to live for.

Assuming you and your guests are normal, choose one of the menus on the following pages.

Be careful. Always check you have the right equipment for the dish – and don't be ambitious. It's always better to achieve great results with a simple theme, than go over the top and risk making a cock-up.

The Drink

First rule, find out who the drivers are and give them Diet Coke, a game of Monopoly, and put them in a separate room. This is kinder to them as they will not be tempted to drink and won't have to endure the sight of their friends enjoying themselves.

For the rest of you, we suggest you start with a champagne cocktail (see page 14). This gets the party off to a good start. If you're poor you can make do

with sparkling wine. Spirits before dinner, we feel, should be avoided, as people can become over-refreshed and talk crap all evening.

It is important to match the wines with the food offered. Generous guests will often bring wine with them, and we think it is only fair that it should be drunk at that meal. So, when you invite your friends, don't be shy about telling them what type of wine to bring. If they're bringing white wine, make sure they chill it well beforehand. If your guests think this is rude, direct them to our Manners section.

The 'Right' Atmosphere

This is the most hit-and-miss element of the party. You can have all the ingredients for a roaring success, and still fail to achieve a mega result. Here are the things to watch out for.

Greeting and Introducing Guests

Always make sure that all your guests are introduced to each other. (The way the Americans do it is a bit naff, e.g. 'Sally, can I introduce you to Bob? He had his fortieth last week, he's just separated from a three-year relationship, but the good news is . . . he's had promotion in the city and a great facelift. Wow!') What a load of rubbish!

The way it should be done is: 'Hey, Sally, meet Bob . . . he's a bit of a dog, so watch out . . .' (*Aside, whispered*: 'He's a bit of a goer!')

Pre-dinner Drinking

This is quite crucial. As you will be in the kitchen overseeing things, make sure someone capable (i.e. with good social skills to keep the conversation going) is in charge of pouring and handing around any nibbles. Nothing new here you might think, but too much beforehand and they'll 'peak' too soon.

Cloakroom Facilities

Always make sure that:

- plenty of loo-roll/towels/soap, etc. are available for your guests.
- coats are hung properly and not just casually thrown on the spare-room bed (as this may be used later during dessert by Sally and Bob).
- there is a functioning lock on the door (loo and bedroom).

Faux Pas and Tantrums

See the Manners section.

Seating

When people don't necessarily know other guests, it is useful to arrange seating so that partners don't sit next to each other (be they straight or gay).

The Table

Don't have a large 'thing' in the middle of the table – this stops all the guests from seeing each other and inhibits conversation. The only exception to this is when you have particularly ugly guests or people who eat with their mouths open and you wish to hide them.

Table linen should be white, and white plates will emphasize the visual impact of the food. Napkins should never be put in a glass. They should be presented neatly, without resorting to some stupid folding nonsense.

Cutlery is arranged with that for the starter on the outside moving in to the main course, pudding spoons and forks at the head of the setting.

Lighting

Traditionally, candles lend atmosphere to the dining experience but one should use plenty of them so that you can actually see what you're eating and what your guests look like. (Naturally, if you have blind guests they can sit in any poorly lit corners, although it is de rigueur to provide white chopsticks for them if Chinese food is served.) Any white or ivory candle is OK – coloured ones (and scented candles or incense sticks) should never be tolerated.

Music

Should be played with a great deal of thought. It should not be intrusive while people are holding a conversation, and is probably best avoided during the actual eating of the meal. However, if you insist on background music then use your common sense to put on selections that will not offend. Loud music is fine after the meal if people wish to dance. If you have black guests, some rap music or reggae might go down well, or bagpipe music if your friends are Scottish.

Planning the Cooking

Now you have your guest list finalized, the next stage is to choose a menu. Creating a range of menus in three sections suits all budgets and ensures that the courses have a degree of 'balance'. Occasionally, dilemmas arise because a guest is a vegetarian or has an eating disorder such as wheat intolerance. Should you make something special for them? The answer is simple . . . no. If the food's going to kill them, let them die . . .

The individual recipes often have guide logos which tell you if cooking preparation may be undertaken in advance. This is useful for the host who wants to spend the maximum time socializing with the guests and the minimum in the kitchen. It should be noted that certain dishes (some terrines and cakes) need to be chilled for a couple of days to allow the flavours to develop. This will help relieve the burden of preparation on the day.

Equipment

If your kitchen is fully equipped you won't have a problem with producing good results. If your equipment is limited, then read the recipes and ensure you are able to provide equivalents for all the recommended utensils. For example, a traditional meshed potato masher will do the job, but a hand-turned mouli-type sieve will make the dish memorable.

Cookers vary widely in their actual performance and the guides given here for temperatures and times may vary depending on the age and efficiency of your oven, hob etc. We recommend buying fridge and oven thermometers to keep a check on the actual temperatures achieved.

All the recipes in this book are specified for eight people with reasonable appetites. As a result, you should pay attention to the size of your utensils: for example, the dessert mould or tart tin you possess may only be big enough for six portions. Rather than have the dilemma of 'Who gets the small portions?', it is better to think ahead than be stingy with your friends.

We have attempted to give ideas for dishes that can be produced without the need for any complicated array of implements. However, we list here a number of efficient kitchen tools that will enhance your ability to get the best results, without having to spend a fortune.

In General

- metal-handled frying pan (for *tartes Tatin*, oven roasts etc.)
- cafetières/espresso coffee machines
- food processor
- electric hand-held whisk (for sauces, soups and dressings)
- electric blender
- hand-turned mouli (coarse- and fine-meshed sieves)
- wok (wooden handle preferred for easy tossing) *
- thermometers (for fridge and oven)
- scallop-edged tongs (for easy manipulation of all types of foods in cooking)
- steamer

* *How to season your wok.*

A traditional steel wok has a light coating of machine oil from the factory to prevent rusting. This has to be scrubbed off with steel wool and strong detergent. After rinsing thoroughly, heat the wok on a high flame until the metal 'blues' and discolours. Move the pan around the flame until all the surface is discoloured and you are sure all traces of any residual coating have been vaporized.

Next allow the wok to cool somewhat so that a light coating of peanut or sunflower oil (or similar) can be smeared over the new surface with kitchen paper. It also will tend to vaporize and give off smoke. The residue, however, will adhere to the pan and 'blacken it up'. Scrub the metal with ground salt and kitchen paper. Rinse with cold water. The wok is now seasoned.

Do not, however, undo all your hard work by washing it in hot soapy water at any time. After cooking just rinse out with cold water when just finished cooking (removing any stubborn bits with a steel wool scrubber). This will keep your wok in perfect condition.

As with all non-stick pans, even the best-quality Teflon surfaces wear and get scratched with time, so we would still recommend a traditional steel wok. Wooden-handled is best, metal ones are too hot to hold and thus difficult to manipulate.

Knives

It is worth spending a reasonable amount of money on steel knives. It is also essential to have a good sharpener. Working with a blunt knife is dangerous because when you are adding more pressure to the blade to do the job, there's more chance of it slipping and causing injury.

Pots and Pans

Stainless-steel or cast-iron (or a combination thereof) are best. Aluminium non-stick pans are OK, but as most people know, they don't last a lifetime.

Ingredients

Modern thinking has changed the accent from complicated sauces and food that has been meddled with to one of simplicity. Now you should strive to get the best quality ingredients and cook and present them as simply as possible. Most traditional cookery books had their antecedents in Victorian kitchens, and they contained strict rules about what sauces could go with what ingredients. The resulting guideline was referred to in cumbersome French, e.g. 'Americaine' meant 'with slices of tomatoes and potatoes, julienne of celery, onions and boiled eggs'; and 'Italienne' meant 'crumbed in the Milanese style, cooked in butter, dressed in a circle garnished centre with artichoke hearts mixed with Italian sauce'. Very formal (and boring) stuff!

The influx of foreign influences such as those of the Mediterranean, Indian and South-East Asian cuisines has dispensed with all this formality and placed the accent firmly back on taste. Thank God.

Each kitchen ingredient has its own special virtue and appropriate use. Always demand the best quality you can get and afford, and practise recipes using them. Everyone appreciates how dull cardboard apples are, and how frozen fish never quite has the texture of fresh. In cooking, when using those ingredients, obey a few simple rules:

– Use fresh herbs wherever possible. A few types of dried herbs lose their whole 'function' once dry, parsley, for instance. Fresh, it adds a subtle finish to many dishes. Dry, it is basically worthless as far as adding 'taste' is concerned.

– Oils will not last for ever, they oxidize and go rancid (the same as butter), so keep your stocks to a minimum.

– Use appropriate olive oils for each task. Virgin is best for dressings; other dishes, such as bruschetta, call for the best quality you can buy – go for an extra virgin from an area known for its premium oils, such as Umbria, Tuscany or Sicily.

– The same goes for spices, which lose their potency with age. Most at risk are ground spices, especially the 'sweet' ones such as nutmeg and mace. These are very aromatic on grinding but will soon deteriorate. Check your spice pots by a judicious sniff at each one. Your nose will tell you which have 'died'. It'll help to keep them in the dark. Buy whole spices wherever possible.

– We always recommend Maldon salt. It gives a clean taste that enhances the food without any bitter aftertaste associated with rock salts and others.

– In desserts that call for chocolate, try to find a product that has a high percentage of cocoa solids. This means that the degree of cocoa mass of the bar is high and will give a good result. Aim for 70% (Cadbury's Bourneville is 50% and will be sufficient).

– Clarified butter is useful for some recipes. It is made by bringing butter briefly to the boil, without browning, and letting the froth settle. Watery buttermilk solids will coagulate at the bottom of the pan. Pour off the hot oily butterfat for use.

– Always go for quality wherever possible and don't hoard. Ingredients don't 'live' for ever.

Planning the Drink

Wine

In Britain, we are fortunate in having no wine industry to speak of. This allows us to be less prejudiced than, say, the French, for example, who think they are the only people on the planet who can make decent wine, giving us the freedom to buy and drink wines from any number of places

As far as choosing wine is concerned, this is down to personal taste and budget. Off-licences and the supermarkets offer a great choice from all over the world, many with a detailed guide to their degree of sweetness/dryness. The down-side of the vast choice is that with so many wines, what do you buy? The answer is, as with anything complicated (such as what car or computer do you buy), research and extensive test-driving. Here are a few guidelines.

Some of those in the 'old-school' wine trade can be rather pompous and stuck up and talk down to anyone who knows less than they do. So, point one: don't be intimidated by this unfortunate breed of salesman. Point two: some of the wine fraternity have gone mad. They say things like the wine is 'musty smelling . . . like the loft . . . with a hint of dry rot'. What nonsense. This is where we need plain English, to give us real advice as to the nature of the wine's flavour and texture. Do you really want to drink something that tastes like the loft? Of course not! Point three: should you drink white wine only with fish and not with meat? Again, this is a matter of taste, but we think it's fair to say that whatever you serve must complement the food in a way that doesn't 'fight' with it. You can drink a chilled Fleurie with fish, for instance. It goes very well, and there is nothing wrong with a full-bodied white with lamb, say, but there is little point in drinking a light white with a curry. When all is said and done, however, it's up to you.

Another question often asked is how long a red wine should be opened before it's ready to serve. The answer is that all reds will improve a little after opening as the air gets to the wine. It starts to 'breathe' on opening and with exposure to air the full flavour will begin to develop. The change is more noticeable in an older rather than a newer wine. As you know, when you go to a restaurant they open the wine as you order it.

Storage of wine is important. Most wine should be left in a cool dark place laid horizontally, on its side. This keeps the cork damp and a damp cork will not shrink and thus let in air (if air gets into a bottle of wine the wine will go off, and a bottle of corked wine is enough to ruin our whole day). More wine producers are using plastic corks for their bottles. So far, this is only available at the cheaper end of the market but, by all accounts, the corks work well.

Beers

Beer is a good drink to have with, say, a curried something with a strong spicy flavour or a chilli-hot item that needs that cold sparkling taste to 'cut through'. So a light lager beer is perfect. A cold beer in the summer with a barbecue can work well with spicy, grilled foods and, of course, the neighbours are always happy to pick up the empty cans that have been thrown over the fence.

Spirits

These should be treated with care at the beginning of a dinner party. Hosts may offer their guests overly-strong vodka and tonics and they are then 'history' for the entire evening, talking nonsense and falling over everything. So go easy on the spirits and build the atmosphere of the party *slowly*. It will then be more fun and the loo won't need redecorating.

Drinks on Arrival

Champagne is perfect to greet guests and helps to get the party going. If your budget stretches to champagne cocktails then here's an elegant recipe.

The Nosh Brothers' Champagne Cocktail

Serves 4

1 bottle champagne (a good-quality dry sparkling
*   wine will do, Mumm Cuvée Napa is ideal)*
juice of 1 lemon
juice of 2 limes
¼ wine glass cassis (good-quality thick crème de
*   cassis)*
½ wine glass calvados
300 ml (½ pint) freshly squeezed chilled orange
*   juice (a fresh-style brand like Tropicana,*
*   without pulp, is good)*

Squeeze the fresh lime and lemon juice into a jug. Add the cassis, calvados, and chilled orange juice, and stir. Half-fill champagne flutes with this mixture and, as your guests arrive, gently top up with the sparkling wine. Cheers!

Drinks after Dinner

Tea should never be offered or drunk at a dinner party. This is one of those new-wave limp-wristed things that is, quite frankly, completely unnecessary. If a guest should give you grief, whining, 'But it's our national drink', simply reply, 'Yes, you're right – at tea-time – that's at 4 o'clock, now bugger off!'

However, coffee is fine, and is important at the end of any meal. The problem is that people think that if they are asked whether or not they want coffee the party may be drawing to a close – so you can use it in one of two ways:

1 To get rid of your guests.
2 To prevent the early departure of your guests due to tiredness. This allows them to be able to drink more and stay longer.

If you are serving coffee it must be fresh and you must have the proper equipment to make it in. Coffee varieties are a matter of personal taste, but if in doubt, get a good-quality Colombian. It is ideal as an after-dinner drink (medium ground for cafetières and fine ground for filters). For espresso machines a dark roast is perfect.

Whilst we prefer the use of 'fully loaded' coffee, we accept that many people cannot drink it late at night. If this is the case, then a good-quality decaff (Lavazza 'blue' pack) is essential.

For people with a real passion for good coffee, we can recommend Torz & Macatonia, gourmet coffee roasters and by appointment to the Nosh Brothers. They mail-order and are on 0171 515 7770.

Only white sugar should be offered, as other sugars taint the flavour of the coffee. If you must offer chocolates with the coffee, then only high-quality dark chocolate should be used.

Manners and Etiquette

Food is a fashion, and each generation has its own guidelines for the mutual enjoyment of the meal. British eating habits are largely inherited from the Victorians and Edwardians who made a big fuss of dos and don'ts. We have no problem with rules that enhance the enjoyment and ritual. However, there seem to be some erstwhile fashions that are now, frankly, a little passé. Most definitely out are: wine baskets, fish cutlery, fondue sets, candles in Chianti bottles, hostess trolleys and leather-studded ice buckets.

Even without these abominations, there exist some definitely dubious and irritating modern habits and faux pas that can raise an eyebrow. They include the following:

Mobile Phones

Should be left switched off unless the guest is a doctor on call, in which case he/she will probably be with the non-drinkers, playing Monopoly in the next room.

Smoking

Considered by most people nowadays to be an anti-social habit. Some hosts forbid smoking altogether. Smoking while eating can be difficult at a fork buffet and ash can pollute the food. If a guest is asked to smoke outside, the good host will always have brollies available should the weather be inclement.

Farting or Belching

If a guest breaks wind loudly he/she should be reprimanded instantly, to act as a deterrent to other potentially 'windy' guests.

Tantrums

Tantrums may range from a guest who arrives slightly over-refreshed to the wife who has just found out about hubby shagging the next-door neighbours' au pair who's blonde, Swedish and fun. Regardless of the cause of the tantrum, you must deal firmly with the problem with varying degrees of threat.

For the drunk who is slightly unmanageable, either send them away or try your best to sober them up and reason with them. If neither works, poison them. For the major marital trauma, ask to see a picture of the Swedish girl and nod approvingly at your guest's good taste, whilst reassuring the wife that her husband has made an unfortunate error of judgement. Offer another champagne cocktail.

Sickness

Throwing up at the table is sometimes unavoidable. But there is an element of etiquette to be aware of in such instances. That is, always throw up white wine with the fish course and red with the meat. This is less unattractive to other guests during eating.

Death

Should a guest die during the party, you should, of course, continue in the next room, leaving the deceased at the table, in peace, to be collected later. If he/she hasn't started a particular course, it *is* fair to arrange for the 'extra' portion to be divided up amongst the remainder of the guests. Naturally, if the deceased's head has fallen on to the dish, it would be bad manners to move the body just to reach the uneaten food (unless, of course, it is a particularly good dish). If there is no alternative room to remove to, then the deceased may be covered up with a suitable cloth or coat, and conversation may be continued. However, although it's OK to talk over the body, it would be bad manners to talk about the person.

Notes for Guests

– Arrive a little after the time you're invited. Never on the dot. Your hosts may still be in the shower and running a little late.

– Try to remember your host's name. It's not so important to remember other guests' names. In fact, if anyone is arrogant and snotty to us, we make a point of calling him or her by a different name each time we address them. (Which gives us a great deal of pleasure . . . soon the other guests latch on to the game, and everyone joins in.)

– Do not arrive over-refreshed, with slurred speech.

— It is imperative that the wine you bring is of premier quality. This will ensure a decent chance for your host to open it at that meal. If the wine you bring is dreadful plonk, the offended host may drop the bottle 'accidentally'. (Note for hosts: it is difficult to get away with this more than once.)

— If your hosts are Muslim, teetotal or just plain mean, bring alcohol with you disguised as fresh orange juice or in a soft drinks bottle. Tell them that it has the medicine for your gout in it – so they don't attempt to drink it and catch you out.

To Get Rid of Guests

— Stop talking to them and stop serving drinks (only water).

— Enquire how they are getting home.

— Offer guests the use of your phone to make a call to a taxi company (dial the number yourself for obvious reasons).

— If it's winter, open the windows to let in some air.

— Make comments like 'Well, it's been fun,' or 'Oh, my God! Is that the time?'

— Go and brush your teeth, leaving the bathroom door open.

— If that doesn't work, start hoovering!

Nosh Symbols

Vegetarian recipe.

Recipe can be prepared in advance.

Be careful! Attention to detail needed.

Particularly rich dish.

Easy foolproof method.

Don't meddle with this recipe.
You have been warned!

Menus for the Poor

Introduction

Just because you don't have an unlimited budget, it doesn't mean you can't put on a spread that will be memorable. This section has been carefully compiled with ideas for maximizing taste without compromising your already strained pockets.

Peasant cooking has, fortunately, been embraced by new English cuisine and has pointed the way to keeping flavour levels high on the Nosh-O-Meter. For instance, cheaper cuts of meat have been used, which will provide the maximum flavour. It is well known to enthusiastic cooks that meat near the bone, although sometimes coarser in texture, often has the sweetest taste. For example, just think how rich oxtail is . . . and that seems mostly bone when you first look at it!

The same is true for fish. Brill, mentioned here, or indeed many other good inshore species, produce superb results . . . you don't need to have the dosh for sea bass to enjoy eating fine fish.

Some of the recipes in the 'rich' section will work equally well with some of their expensive elements substituted by cheaper types of ingredient – for example, blinis with salmon eggs (keta) are great, if you can't afford Beluga caviar. But don't make the mistake of substituting cheaper *quality* ingredients. It is better to use quality produce and, say, create the recipe with mussels, rather than skimping on the oils and other bits and trying to keep the langoustine.

If you don't understand this principle, buy baked beans and then gamble on the National Lottery. Then if you really hit the jackpot, you can employ us to come around and cook for you directly.

MENU 1

Spinacci con salsiccia *with garlic toasts*

Spaghetti carbonara Romana

Simple apple tart

MENU 2

Tortilla with peppers, mushrooms, chorizo and peas

Pan-fried brill fillets with gremolata

Apple strudel with liqueur cream

MENU 3

Warm salad of field mushrooms, black pudding, sauté potatoes and tapenade

Chicken breasts with Puy lentils, pancetta and herbs

Lemon mousse

MENU 4

Leek and Roquefort tart with salad

Continental sausages with sauerkraut and boiled potatoes

Lemon pancakes with liqueur orange sauce

MENU 5

*Fettucine with tomato and basil sauce and
moon-dried tomatoes*

Braised beef with red wine, mushrooms and shallots

*Bread and butter pudding with orange and
lemon zest*

MENU 6

*Baby spinach with smoked lardons, avocado and
warm honey dressing*

*Roast fillet of pork with a mustard and
macadamia nut crust*

Pear tarte Tatin

MENU 7

*Chilled vichyssoise with parsley pesto and
garlic croutons*

Mussels with shallots, white wine and herbs

Strawberry ice with tuile biscuits

MENU 8

Crostini with roasted red peppers and basil

Risotto of squids in their ink

Peaches in dessert wine

MENU 9

Smoked chicken with moon-dried tomatoes

*Bavette of beef with braised potato and
onion in beer*

Crème caramel with Stroh rum

MENU 10

*Greek salad of home-made feta cheese, tomato,
cucumber and Kalamata olives*

*Roast belly of pork with caramelized apple,
parsnips and bubble and squeak*

Chocolate mousse with Cointreau

Spinacci con salsiccia with garlic toasts

Spinacci con salsiccia means simply 'spinach with sausage'. We have to own up to stealing this starter from a favourite restaurant in London, but we've improved it, so that's acceptable behaviour. Spinach, lightly wok-fried until wilted, makes a starter, and is substantial enough for a quick meal.

You will need a wok, preferably round-bottomed, on a high gas flame to cook this dish. If you want to save time, you can pre-cook the sausage meat by stir-frying it around the pan for a few minutes, letting it cool, then covering with clingfilm and chilling for cooking with later.

Garlic toasts
3 garlic cloves, peeled
3 tbsp extra-virgin olive oil
8 thick slices ciabatta bread

Spinach with sausages
3 tbsp olive oil
5 salsiccia 'piccante', skins removed and meat crumbled *
1.4 kg (3 lb) baby spinach, washed and de-stalked
sea salt
3 tbsp good-quality balsamic vinegar

* These heavily spiced Italian sausages can be bought from good delis and are distinguished by being tied into links with brown sisal string, with speckled coarse black pepper visible through the skins.

Method

Crush the garlic into the extra-virgin olive oil and paint it on to one side of the ciabatta slices. Grill under a hot flame to brown the bread and create garlic toasts.

Meanwhile, heat the wok all over the surface for some minutes until you see the metal 'blue' (this shows you it is very hot). Then add half the olive oil. (If you try to cook everything in one go, you'll end up cooling down the pan too much and stewing it, so cook in two or three lots.) When the oil is smoking hot, toss in the sausage meat and fry for a few minutes until cooked. Throw in large bunches of spinach, tossing and turning it around the wok to wilt it. When all the greens have been incorporated, season with salt and deglaze with a few splashes of balsamic vinegar. The resulting mix can be placed over the hot garlic toast and served immediately while still piping hot.

Spaghetti carbonara Romana

Spaghetti carbonara is a favourite, but do as we say or you'll end up with scrambled egg. Also don't stint on the ingredients or it will taste like it came out of a can – and we don't tolerate that sort of behaviour.

8 large spring onions, chopped
8 garlic cloves, peeled
8 tbsp olive oil
150 ml (¼ pint) white wine
a generous handful of chopped parsley

5 eggs

900 ml (1½ pints) single cream

sea salt and ground white pepper

150 g (5 oz) Parmesan, finely grated

350 g (12 oz) Parma ham or smoked ham, rind
    and fat discarded, cut into fine strips*

1 kg (2¼ lb) fresh spaghetti or capellini**

a knob of butter

To serve

freshly ground black pepper

finely grated Reggiano Parmesan

* *The slices of Parma ham from the 'ankle' (the
narrow end of the ham) are perfect.*

** *Capellini, or angel hair pasta, is also very good
and gives a lighter result. Sometimes called spaghettini.*

Method

In a large high-sided frying pan, sauté the chopped
spring onions with the whole garlic cloves in olive oil
for a few minutes on a medium high heat. Do not let
them brown. Remove the garlic and discard. Then,
taking the pan off the heat, add the white wine and
parsley, and let the pan cool.

Whisk the eggs into the cream, add seasoning, and
pour into the pan. Stir around rapidly taking care
that the mixture does not 'set' at any point on the
bottom (it won't if the pan has completely cooled).
Add the cheese and ham, and let rest.

Cook the pasta for between about 4 and 6 minutes,
depending on its type and moisture content. Ensure
it is kept at a fast boil in plenty of salted water. When
drained, you can add a knob of butter to stop the
strands sticking together in the colander.

Quickly add the hot pasta to the egg mix pan,
folding all the cream sauce into the strands to incor-
porate evenly. Now return immediately to the stove
on a very low heat and keep turning and stirring

the contents to heat and mix it up. The gentle heat
should thicken the sauce. Do not leave to get lumpy
(if the heat is up too high you'll end up with scrambled egg in the pan!), but fold over until the sauce is
clinging to every strand. You should aim for a result
that is moist but not runny. If cooked too long it
will dry and be ruined. Serve with freshly ground
black pepper and plenty of finely grated Reggiano
Parmesan.

DESSERT 1

Simple apple tart

You will need a metal baking tin, round and deep-
sided if possible, approximately 30 cm (12 in) in
diameter.

*1 large pack (about 225 g / 8 oz) fresh flaky pastry
    (frozen is OK)*

12 eating apples (Braeburn are good)

lemon juice

110 g (4 oz) caster sugar

To serve

120 ml (4 fl oz) calvados (apple brandy)

clotted cream

Method

Roll out the pastry to a thickness of about 3 mm
(⅛ in). Cut into a disc 2.5 cm (1 in) wider than the
tin, place on a floured plate and chill in the fridge.

Meanwhile, peel and core the apples, keeping them
in lemon water to stop discoloration. Cut into slices
about 3 mm (⅛ in) thick. Drain and dry. Place the
chilled disc of pastry into the floured baking tin
leaving 1 cm (½ in) turned up at the edge. Place
the apples in a spiral from the middle outwards, with

the thin edge down, *to cover the bottom part of the pastry completely.* Cover the fruit with the caster sugar, sprinkling it on evenly. Slide the tin into a hot (200°C/400°F/Gas 6) oven for about 10–15 minutes until the pastry has risen and is cooked through. Keep an eye on it to ensure the pastry doesn't burn around the edge. If the pastry has cooked but the apples don't have that caramelized look, quickly flash the pan under a very hot grill to get the right colour.

Serve immediately with a heated and flamed ladle of calvados poured over the tart and lots of cream.

Tortilla with peppers, mushrooms, chorizo and peas

Traditionally, a tortilla (or Spanish potato omelette) has only eggs and potato, but we have expanded the dish so that it has the same filling nature but more depth on the flavour front. This is a dish typical of the new wave of Modern British food. We're sure we probably stole this from someone ('*Yes, I remember . . . we did!*' – Mick). It's easy to make, though, and your guests will think you got it at Marks and Sparks. Not a bad thing sometimes.

8 large eggs
2 egg yolks
2 tbsp double cream

sea salt and ground white pepper
450 g (1 lb) waxy new potatoes
4 tbsp olive oil
1 knob salted butter
*110 g (4 oz) chorizo sausage, sliced and diced (optional)**
1 small Spanish onion (or ½ large one), peeled and chopped
1 red pepper, cored, de-seeded and sliced into small chunks
2 garlic cloves, peeled and crushed
110 g (4 oz) button mushrooms, cleaned and roughly sliced
a sprinkling of dried oregano or herbes de Provence
*110 g (4 oz) blanched fresh peas (frozen will do if not in season)***
freshly ground black pepper

* *You can, if desired, leave out the sausage and make the dish vegetarian (God help us). Even so, it is still substantial enough to have a place in this book!*

** *Generally speaking, freezing vegetables changes their nature for the worse, but in this particular dish, we don't mind using them – the taste 'blends in' with all the other veg, and they conveniently 'fill-in' the gaps in the pan!*

Method

Beat the whole eggs lightly with the egg yolks and cream, then season with salt and white pepper. Allow to come to room temperature before cooking.

Parboil the new potatoes in their jackets and set aside to cool. Remove skins and thinly slice.

Heat a solid-based frying pan (cast-iron is good) to medium hot, pour in the olive oil and allow to heat up for a few seconds. Sizzle in the butter, then add the peeled, parboiled potatoes and fry until lightly browned with the chopped chorizo. Then add the onion, pepper and garlic and fry until softened, taking care not to break up the potato when stirring. Add the mushrooms and continue cooking until their juices are running out and then reduce the heat to low, ensuring all the juices are 'cooking into' the vegetables. (If the mushrooms are not cooked enough, the juices will continue to leak out into the egg mix later and the omelette will not set properly.) Now season the mix with a sprinkling of herbs, salt and white pepper and fold in the peas.

Flatten the vegetables in the pan lightly and pour over the egg mix. Cook on low for about 5 minutes, ensuring the mixture is evenly distributed and that the hob does not brown one side more than the other. After 5 minutes the mixture should be almost set and you can finish it off by placing the pan under a medium-hot grill to set the top. The final result should be about 2 cm (1½ in) in depth with the middle moist and firm but not runny. Sprinkle with black pepper.

The best way to serve the omelette is to leave it to rest for some while to set fully. Then it is easier to cut and serve. Also, the subtle nature of the flavours is more prominent when it is tepid. In fact, in Spain this is a dish that is perfectly acceptable to serve from cold.

MAIN COURSE 2

Pan-fried brill fillets with gremolata

Suggested accompaniment
Fennel (see page 144)

Brill is a common coastal flatfish from around the shores of Britain that has both a fine texture and flavour. It is generally inexpensive, and the gremolata on top just adds that little bit of originality.

Gremolata is a 'dry' dressing of finely chopped parsley, lemon zest and very finely chopped garlic. Parsley only retains its freshness for a few hours before it dies and gives a rank aroma, like old hay, so always prepare the gremolata last and make it freshly each meal – it does not keep.

You will need a pan that does not have a plastic or wooden handle.

Gremolata
2 tbsp finely chopped parsley
1 garlic clove, peeled and very finely chopped
zest of 2 lemons

Fish
4 medium brill (to make 8 fillets)
plain flour and polenta for dredging *
4 tbsp olive oil
4 garlic cloves, peeled but whole
2 shallots, peeled and finely chopped
175 ml (6 fl oz) white wine for deglazing
lemon oil **
sea salt and ground white pepper

* To the plain flour for dredging, add sea salt and white pepper to season. Then, add some fine flour (Italian maize flour) in a proportion of 4:1 flour-to-polenta. Polenta has a coarser texture than wheat flour and adds a robust texture to the fine grade of the fish flesh.

** You can buy lemon-infused olive oil ready for pouring but it's easily made at home – see page 153.

Method

To prepare the gremolata, simply mix the ingredients together.

Preheat the oven to 200°C/400°F/Gas 6.

Although brill is quite a small fish it is unlikely you will have a pan large enough to pan-fry eight fillets at a time so divide them into two batches of four. The fillets are quite small, cook quickly and you won't therefore have to spend a lot of time hanging around. Dredge the fillets with the seasoned flour mix and shake off the excess. Heat half the olive oil until medium hot, add a couple of garlic cloves and half the chopped shallots, and pan-fry four of the fillets presentation-side down first for about a minute or until the surface is light golden-brown in places. Add half the wine. There will be a considerable sizzle as the alcohol steams and boils off. Discard the garlic cloves and then place the pan into the hot oven for about 3 minutes to cook the fish right through. If desired, you can turn the fillets over, and continue to cook on the hob, but the oven method means less handling, and therefore less chance of the delicate fillets breaking up. Repeat with the remaining oil, garlic, shallots, brill and wine.

To serve, slide a fillet on to each plate, pour over the fish juices from the pan, and then (with your thumb over the spout) sprinkle with a few drops of lemon oil, freshly ground black pepper and the gremolata.

Fennel is a good accompaniment to this dish. The fish fillets can be placed on the dish with the fennel around them and the juices poured over all the dish evenly.

DESSERT 2

Apple strudel with liqueur cream

For the last course the men should change into their leather shorts and put on those stupid feathered hats as we magic our way to Austria for a little strudel. A word of warning – if you make our strudel as we say, it is fantastic. It you screw around with the method, it will not turn out well, so you've been warned! (We were only following orders.)

This type of dessert had its origins in Ottoman cuisine from the Middle East, but over the centuries migrated through into Europe and, like the croissant (literally, 'crescent'), found its home in Vienna and helped create the traditional dessert patisserie that we recognize as an Austrian tradition today.

1.4 kg (3 lb) Bramley cooking apples
juice of 1 lemon, squeezed halves retained
2 cloves
1 small cinnamon stick
110 g (4 oz) caster sugar
zest of 1 orange
50 g (2 oz) sultanas
80 g (3 oz) unsalted butter, melted
1 large packet fresh filo (strudel) pastry *

   To serve
icing sugar
whipping cream mixed with kirsch (cherry
   eau-de-vie) to taste

* Try to get about six layers of filo per dessert. Too little and there will be not enough to cover the fruit. Too many layers, and the inner ones will not cook crisply through and will taste papery and 'wet' in the middle.

Method

Preheat the oven to 200–225°C/400–425°F/Gas 6–7.

Peel and core the apples, placing them in water with the squeezed lemon halves to avoid discoloration. Drain the apples well, then chop.

Put the lemon juice, apples, spices, sugar, orange zest and sultanas into a suitable pan. Cook on a low heat, stirring frequently to prevent sticking, and to encourage the juices to emerge from the apple as it cooks down. The resulting stewed fruit mix should be quite stiff, with some chunks of apple visible, and not be a sloppy purée, otherwise it will not fill the strudel leaves easily. Take care, Bramleys will go to pulp easily if you overcook them.

When the fruit is ready, after about 5–8 minutes or so, butter each of the leaves of filo, placing one on top of each other in layers, and fill with the apple mixture in a long log down the central line of the pastry. Then fold the leaves of filo over the top of the fruit * and create a log of pastry, tucking the ends of the filo inside the fold at each end. The butter brushed on will tend to congeal as it cools and form a glue seal that should prevent any fruit escaping.

* *You may like to remove the cloves and cinnamon stick prior to baking.*

When the filling is already done, you only need to place the strudel in the oven, outside surface buttered generously, for 5–6 minutes or so until browned in places. It is possible to make smaller individual 'parcels' of strudel, but you will need to watch the timing more closely to prevent over-baking.

Don't assemble the strudel 'log' or 'parcels' more than 15 minutes before it is time for baking – otherwise the filo will get waterlogged and mushy.

The hot strudel can be dusted with icing sugar and then cut into sections to be served with kirsch cream.

Warm salad of field mushrooms, black pudding, sauté potatoes and tapenade

Black pudding, or blood sausage as it is sometimes known, is traditionally a Northern thing. It's also served around Europe, and is known as *morcilla* in Spain, *Blutwurst* in Germany, *boudin noir* in France and *drisheen* in Ireland. We mention this, because your guests may take the piss over the fact that you're serving black pudding at a dinner party, but we think it's quite chic.

Tapenade
1 small can anchovies, drained
3 garlic cloves, peeled and chopped
1 small jar pitted black olives (Greek Kalamatas are good)
1 small jar pickled caper berries, drained
2 tbsp virgin olive oil

Salad
a selection of crisp salad leaves (e.g. oakleaf, lamb's lettuce, frisée, escarole, batavia, etc.)
450 g (1 lb) old potatoes, peeled and parboiled
25 g (1 oz) butter
4 tbsp olive oil
450 g (1 lb) spicy black pudding sliced into 5 mm (¼ in) thick rounds
2 shallots, peeled and chopped
*4 large open field mushrooms (*Agaricus campestris*), sliced thin across the cap*
vinaigrette for salad dressing (see page 154)

freshly ground black pepper
2 tbsp chopped parsley

Tapenade method

Place the ingredients in a food processor and blitz on pulse for a few short bursts. You should not purée the mix, but end up with a pâté-like mix that has a coarse oily texture.

Salad method

Wash, pick and mix the salad in equal quantities and rest in a chilled bowl.

Pan-fry the potatoes until browned in the butter and half the olive oil, and then add the black pudding and chopped shallots and continue to cook for a few minutes until done. Add the mushrooms and cook until some juices come out.

Toss the salad in a large bowl with enough vinaigrette to coat the leaves evenly. Place a cone-shaped pile of leaves on each starter plate and place a few spoonfuls of the sausage/potato/mushroom mix on and around the pile. Place neatly without crushing the pile but do not arrange too fussily. This is a peasant-style dish and should look appropriately rustic.

The olive tapenade can then be sprinkled on and around the plate off a small teaspoon. It has a strong taste and should be used sparingly. Finally, dress the salad with black pepper and parsley.

Chicken breasts with Puy lentils, pancetta and herbs

Suggested accompaniment
Mashed potato with soured cream and spring onions
(see page 147)

The next dish sounds like it could be for hippies and veggies – who else would bother to eat lentils – but with herbs and pancetta we noshed it up, serving it with chicken. It tastes darn good.

Lentils
600 g (1 lb 5 oz) Puy lentils (small green lentils)
2 medium onions, peeled
2 garlic cloves, peeled
2 large ripe tomatoes, skinned
110 g (4 oz) pancetta (Italian smoked belly bacon)
2 tbsp olive oil
50 g (2 oz) unsalted butter
freshly chopped parsley
fresh thyme leaves
2 bay leaves
chicken stock (see page 155)
sea salt and freshly ground black pepper

Chicken
8 × 175 g (6 oz) free-range boneless chicken breasts
6 tbsp olive oil
salt and ground white pepper
120 ml (4 fl oz) white wine
150 ml (¼ pint) chicken stock (reduced from 450 ml (¾ pint), see page 155)

Lentil method

Pour boiling water over the lentils and soak them while preparing the other ingredients. Finely (and separately) chop the onions, garlic, tomatoes and the bacon. Drain the lentils and heat the oil and half the butter in a sauté pan. Fry the chopped onion for a couple of minutes with half the chopped bacon, then add the drained lentils and the garlic. Stir to mix, then add the tomatoes and herbs, and cover with a light chicken stock to a depth of 2.5 cm (1 in). Bring to the boil, then simmer for 25 minutes and season. The lentils should be soft but not mushy with a slight bite to them (add a dash of water or stock if they are dryish but too hard).

When the lentils are done, fry the remaining bacon until crisp, and drain on kitchen paper.

Remove any herb stalks and leaves, swirl in the remaining butter and sprinkle with the bacon bits.

Chicken method

Preheat the oven to 200–225°C/400–425°F/Gas 6–7.

The chicken method is simple. Place the oiled sea-soned breasts in a pan, presentation-side down, over a high heat, and turn when browned (about 5 minutes). Deglaze with the white wine and keep the heat on full for a few minutes to allow the wine and juices to reduce. Add the reduced chicken stock to the pan and place in the oven for 5 minutes. To test if the breasts are done, prick the underside with a sharp metal skewer – if the juices run out clear the chicken is done. If they are still very pink, then return to the oven for a few minutes more.

To serve

Place the lentils on a warm plate with the chicken breasts on top and cover the meat with the strong chicken juices.

DESSERT 3

Lemon mousse

6 eggs, separated
110 g (4 oz) caster sugar
4 sheets gelatine (or small packet) *
250 ml (8 fl oz) whipping cream
juice and zest of 2 lemons

* *This is for 'English' produced gelatine – increase to 7 sheets if it is 'continental', as the sheets are thinner.*

Method

Beat the egg yolks and sugar together until white and fluffy. Roll the gelatine sheets, put them into a tall glass and cover with cold water. Leave for 5 minutes until limp, then melt in a pan in a bain-marie in a little water. When completely dissolved, add to the egg/sugar mixture.

Whisk the egg whites until soft peaks form. Whip the cream and mix into the whisked egg whites. Thoroughly mix half of this in to the egg/sugar mixture with the juice and zest, and fold in the rest gently. Put into individual serving dishes, cover and chill.

STARTER 4

Leek and Roquefort tart with salad

Leek and Roquefort tart is lovely served with some warm crispy French bread, some unsalted butter and a bottle or two of white burgundy. It makes a great starter or is just the thing for a lunch. However, if you're still hungry, then the next thing on the menu will certainly fill the gap.

Because of the cooking time and temperature needed for the sausages, you will need to make this dish in advance, warming before serving.

You'll need a large springform tart tin for this dish – about 20–23 cm (8–9 in) in diameter should be enough; preferably it should have 7.5 cm (3 in) high sides, which makes for a good deep tart. You'll also need baking beans and greaseproof paper.

Rich shortcrust pastry
175 g (6 oz) plain flour
a pinch of salt
110 g (4 oz) unsalted butter, cut into small dice
2 egg yolks
2 tbsp grated Parmesan
2 tbsp cold water
butter or sunflower oil, for greasing

Filling
450 g (1 lb) small leeks, trimmed, washed and finely chopped
25 g (1 oz) unsalted butter
4 shallots, peeled and finely chopped
6 egg yolks

600 ml (1 pint) single cream
sea salt, ground white pepper and freshly ground black pepper
225 g (8 oz) Roquefort cheese

Salad
225 g (8 oz) mixed strong leaves
walnut dressing (see page 154)

Tart method

Prepare the pastry. Sift the flour and salt into a bowl, then add the butter dice. Rub the mixture between your fingers until it resembles breadcrumbs. Add the egg yolks, Parmesan and water to bind into a firm mix. Place in the fridge for half an hour to chill. This ensures the pastry will roll well, will not crack when moulded into the tart tin, and will not sag when placed in the oven to bake blind.

When chilled, roll the pastry out to a thickness of 3 mm (⅛ in), and use to line a tin greased with butter or sunflower oil. Some pastry should stand 'proud' of the top of the dish. Line the tin with silicone baking parchment and cover the base of the tin with baking beans. Place in a medium hot oven (190°C/375°F/Gas 5) for 10–15 minutes to bake blind. (The beans stop the bottom surface from 'bubbling up' and distorting the shape.) When cool enough to touch, remove the beans and paper, and allow the pastry case to cool while cooking the filling.

For the filling, sauté the leeks in the butter with the shallots until soft. Beat the egg yolks into the cream, season with white pepper and salt, and crumble in the Roquefort cheese. Add the leek/shallot mixture and pour carefully into the tart casing. Bake for about 25–30 minutes in an oven preheated to 180°C/350°F/Gas 4.

Serve hot or at least warm, in wedges, with the mixed dressed salad leaves and sprinkled with black pepper.

Salad method

The tart is quite savoury with the strong cheese flavour and you can use some strong salad materials accordingly, e.g. cos, oakleaf, escarole, red batavia, pissenlit blanc (blanched dandelion), frisée and rocket. Use any radicchio sparingly. Add the walnut dressing to taste.

MAIN COURSE 4

Continental sausages with sauerkraut and boiled potatoes

Mick once ordered this dish during the height of a Parisian summer heatwave at Chez Hansi, a kitschly-decorated Swiss/Alsacien-style restaurant in Montparnasse, whilst dining alone. Ordering the dish extravagantly in poor French from the hand-written menu, he failed to notice the item was *pour deux personnes.* It was only when the waiter revealed the huge meal from under a silver cloche with an amused grin and an arrogant shout of '*Voila!*' and 'Monsieur order this, yes?' that Mick realized what he had done. Keeping a straight face, the waiter was told 'Of course, it was deliberate,' and to 'Get me some bloody bread' as a side order as Mick was 'very hungry'. He had to finish the feast – about 1.4 kg or 3 lb of meat and the same of potatoes with a mountain of sauerkraut – in order not to lose face! It was tough as this is a very substantial winter dish and filling at the best of times. Needless to say, he did finish it, feeling pleased to have not embarrassed himself, but had to skip pudding and sleep it off in the car for a few hours.

Should you have any 'lippy' French house guests, shut them up with a dose of their own medicine!

> *2.25 kg (5 lb) sauerkraut, bottled or canned*
> *1 onion, peeled and finely chopped*
> *110 g (4 oz) goose fat*
> *1 pig's trotter, split and blanched **
> *450 g (1 lb) smoked belly of pork*
> *675 g (1½ lb) salt pork, soaked and blanched*
> *2 bay leaves*
> *3 garlic cloves, peeled*
> *6 black peppercorns*
> *3 cloves*
> *1 bottle dry white wine*
> *450 ml (¾ pint) chicken stock (see page 155)*
> *1.6 kg (3½ lb) old floury potatoes*
> *salt*
> *4 Bockwurst sausages*
> *2 Toulouse sausages*
> *1 tbsp olive oil*
> *4 white veal sausages*
> *2 black pudding sausages* (boudins noir*)*

* *Make sure you wash the trotter well before blanching it, as it could have trodden in something! But don't worry: trotters do usually come well cleaned and ready-blanched for the pot.*

Sauerkraut method

Drain off the liquid and wash the sauerkraut in plenty of cold water. Drain and squeeze well, to remove any remaining liquids.

In a large cast-iron casserole pot sweat off the chopped onion in the goose fat. After softening the onion, layer half the sauerkraut on top, then spread the trotter, pork, seasonings and spices on that and cover with the remaining sauerkraut. Pour over the wine and chicken stock, place the lid on and cook in a low (160°C/325°F/Gas 3) oven for 2 hours.

Potato method

Prepare the potatoes for boiling in salted water, allowing 30 minutes before the sauerkraut is ready for serving. Drain when tender.

Sausage method

Some 40 minutes before the sauerkraut is ready, poach the Bockwurst and Toulouse sausages in near boiling water.* Oil the veal sausages and black puddings and grill for 5 minutes under a medium-hot grill.

Don't let the water boil or the sausage skins will split and their contents will burst out.

To serve

Check the casserole contents before serving, discarding any chewy spices like the bay and cloves, and adjusting seasoning as necessary.

Pick the bones off the trotter and from the pork pieces, and discard. Slice the meats and fold back into the 'kraut. Slice the sausages. Arrange a large oval dish with the sauerkraut and sliced chunks of sausages mixed in with the potatoes in a pile in the middle. A good strong Dijon mustard is the only accompaniment needed for this dish.

Lemon pancakes with liqueur orange sauce

An easy dessert to do, as you can make the pancakes in advance, and combine them with the sauce later, when needed. A version of this – crêpes Suzette – was very much in vogue in the early 1960s in restaurants and hotels in the UK, and it fell out of fashion as we began to question French supremacy in the kitchen and stopped copying the Parisian hotel restaurants. Not surprising, given the flashy treatment of being flambéed at the table, which simply burnt off the flavour of the alcohol and added nothing to the overall appeal. A shame, as it really is a classic dish that has lots of appeal for everyone.

In our version we have added lemon zest to the batter which gives it an extra bite to balance the sticky sweetness of the liqueur sauce.

Pancake batter
175 g (6 oz) plain flour
3 eggs
a pinch of sea salt
25 g (1 oz) caster sugar
350 ml (12 fl oz) whole milk
120 ml (4 fl oz) single cream
2 tbsp clarified butter
finely grated zest of 3 lemons
1 tbsp Grand Marnier liqueur

Sauce
225 g (8 oz) unsalted butter, softened
225 g (8 oz) caster sugar
5 tbsp Grand Marnier liqueur
finely grated zest and juice of 2 oranges
peel of 2 oranges, blanched and candied *

* *Using a fine peeler, remove long strips of orange peel (skin only, not the bitter white pith). Cut into fine long strips, 3 mm (⅛ in) wide, and blanch in boiling water for 30 seconds. Then simmer the peel in a sugar syrup (4 tbsp caster sugar dissolved in 150 ml (¼ pint) water) for 5–10 minutes to candy the peel. Remove and add to the sauce when ready.*

Pancake method

Prepare the batter with a hand whisk or blitz in a blender – simply put all the ingredients in a bowl together. The important thing is to let the batter rest at room temperature for about an hour to let the glutens 'emerge' from the flour and homogenize the batter.

To cook the pancakes, simply heat a solid-based iron or steel pan (previously seasoned with oil burnt off and rubbed clean with salt and kitchen paper—as you would with a wok — to prevent sticking) to medium heat. Brush the pan with a little extra melted butter and pour in a small amount of batter to cover the base thinly. Cook for about 1½ minutes or so until the batter appears dry then, using a palette knife, turn the pancake over and cook on the other side for about another 1 minute until golden in colour. Slide the pancake out of the pan on to a cool smooth surface and allow to cool. When cold, place on a cold plate and stack the other pancakes on top. Do not stack pancakes when still hot or even warm as the butter in them will solidify them together and the stack will not peel apart when the crucial time comes.

Sauce method

Work the softened butter into the sugar, then add the Grand Marnier and orange zest. Heat the orange juice in a shallow frying pan (copper pans are good for this as they function well at low temperatures), and simmer to reduce the volume by half.

Beat the butter/sugar mix into the reduced juice, bring it lightly to the boil, then add the candied peel. As the sauce bubbles, lift one pancake at a time into the sauce, spreading it and then folding with the palette knife into quarters. Reserve on a hot plate until the others are done. Allow three pancakes per portion.

STARTER 5

Fettucine with tomato and basil sauce and moon-dried tomatoes

Fettucine with tomatoes and basil is a traditional Italian dish. We have added what are called moon-dried tomatoes to give that extra dimension of flavour and texture.

Tomato and basil sauce
6 × 400 g (14 oz) cans Italian plum tomatoes with their juices
175 ml (6 fl oz) olive oil
1 large Spanish onion, peeled and finely chopped
6 large garlic cloves
1 large bunch fresh sweet basil (about 50 g/2 oz)
2 tbsp fresh or dried oregano
½ tsp ground white pepper
1 heaped tbsp caster sugar
2 tsp sea salt
freshly ground black pepper
25 g (1 oz) unsalted butter

Pasta

450 g (1 lb) fresh fettuccine

salt and freshly ground black pepper

50 g (2 oz) unsalted butter, chopped into small
    chunks

8 moon-dried tomatoes, halved (see page 148)

To serve

freshly grated Parmesan

Sauce method

Pass the tomatoes through a fine mouli sieve to remove seeds and skin.

Heat the olive oil in a solid-based saucepan over a medium heat and add the onion, whole garlic, basil (including the stalks), oregano and white pepper. Stir briskly to prevent browning of the onion. When the onion has softened, add the tomato pulp. Bring the mixture to the boil and immediately reduce the heat to a low simmer. Remove the garlic and discard.

Stir in the sugar (this balances the acidity of the tomatoes) and half of the salt. Simmer the sauce for about half an hour or so until well reduced. The solids will tend to condense on the bottom of the pan, so stir with a wooden spoon occasionally. The time taken for this process will vary depending on the degree of wateriness of the original canned tomato contents, so keep an eye on it.

When the sauce is finished it should be tested for seasoning.* Add the freshly ground black pepper, and the butter to give it a good shine.

* *Remember, as the tomato sauce reduces in volume, the degree of saltiness does too, so don't adjust the final seasoning until the end of the reduction process.*

Pasta method

Cook the fresh pasta in your largest pot in lots of boiling, well salted water. About 4 minutes is usually enough, but test a strand for texture towards the end of boiling. It should have some bite to it. Pour into a large colander and drain well. Return the pasta to the saucepan, add the butter and stir it well in to coat the strands evenly.* Toss in the moon-dried tomatoes and ladle the hot tomato and basil sauce over the fettucine to coat evenly.

* *Even with the pasta buttered, the latent heat in the pasta will cook on as it stands, so serve it immediately before the sauce is absorbed and the pasta turns dry. The sauce should be reduced and heated well so that it clings to the pasta and does not spread out on the dish as a watery pool.*

To serve

Using large tongs lift out and measure equal portions of the pasta into serving bowls. The Parmesan can either be grated on (or served on the table in a separate side dish) or, for a really rustic feel, shaved on in thin long strips using a vegetable peeler.

MAIN COURSE 5

Braised beef with red wine, mushrooms and shallots

Suggested accompaniment
Savoy cabbage (see page 151)
Boiled or mashed potatoes (see page 147)

Braising beef is a good way of making a less expensive cut taste great, and done properly it is very tender. It can be cooked the day before. It's ideal for Sunday lunch, especially if you plan to get trashed on Saturday night – cooking with a hangover can be less than fun.

6 rashers smoked streaky bacon, rind removed
5 tbsp olive oil
2 large Spanish onions, peeled and finely chopped
1 tbsp brown sugar
450 g (1 lb) small shallots, peeled, left whole
1.8 kg (4 lb) shin of beef (untrimmed weight)
3 tbsp plain flour
sea salt and ground white pepper
225 g (8 oz) small button mushrooms, washed
   and halved
2 garlic cloves, peeled and crushed
1 bottle robust red wine (e.g. Fitou)
1 bouquet garni (bay, rosemary, thyme, etc.)
zest and juice of 1 small orange
300 ml (½ pint) beef stock (see page 155)

To serve
freshly ground black pepper
freshly chopped parsley

Method

Trim the large edge of bacon fat off the rashers, chop this into small dice and fry slowly on a low heat in 2 tbsp of the oil until the fat releases its juices and is rendered down. Then add the onions, raise the heat to medium and cook on for about 5 minutes, adding the sugar, until the onions are browned. Don't worry about overdoing the onions – a small amount of slightly 'burnt' edges to the onion lends itself quite well to this particular dish. Remove the onions and reserve.

Now slice the bacon into narrow strips and pan-fry until it starts to turn crisp, then remove with a slotted spoon and reserve with the onions. Add the remaining oil to the pan and brown the whole shallots over a high heat until they are coloured up dark brown, but are not cooked through. Drain, remove and reserve.

Next, trim the beef, removing any sinewy membranes, and cut into large steak-size pieces.* Lightly coat the beef pieces with lightly seasoned flour, shaking off any excess. Keeping the heat on a high flame, brown a couple of pieces of beef at a time. Do not be tempted to fill the pan with meat or the temperature will be drastically lowered and the steaks will leak juices instead of being sealed.

* *Cheaper cuts of beef, like the shin used here, benefit from slow, even cooking. The mistake some people make is to buy very lean-looking cuts (which appeal to the eye on the butcher's display, but don't have enough fat marbled throughout), and cut the meat into pieces that are too small. On cooking this has the effect of drying out the flesh and giving a stringy unappealing result.*

Cook the mushrooms briefly with the garlic, and reserve. Now, deglaze any residues left in the pan with a couple of dashes of the red wine. Fill a casserole with layers of onion, bacon, meat, mushrooms, the remainder of the wine, the bouquet garni, orange juice and zest and the stock. Put a lid (or foil) over the top and place in a medium hot oven (180°C/ 350°F/Gas 4) for about an hour, and then add the shallots over the top. Cook for a further 1–1½ hours until the meat is soft, but not falling apart.

Drain the juices off (discarding the bouquet garni) and reduce in a saucepan at a rolling boil by about half to two-thirds its original volume until it has a dense consistency. The taste should be rich, and the gravy should be able to coat the back of a spoon. Adjust the seasoning if necessary, adding freshly ground black pepper, and return the juices to the casserole. This dish is finished off with a sprinkling of freshly chopped parsley.

Bread and butter pudding with orange and lemon zest

Another memory from school days that can be improved by some degree of attention to detail. Do you remember how they put raisins on top of the pudding? Inevitably, it was baked too hot and the result was that the raisins were burnt black and hard and tasted bitter, making them inedible. Nevertheless, this is a classic English pudding that can still be memorable.

300 ml (½ pint) whole milk
8 tbsp vanilla sugar (see page 152)
8 egg yolks
300 ml (½ pint) single cream
zest of 2 oranges and 3 lemons
a dash of cognac
a handful of raisins
1 loaf sliced white bread, crusts cut off
225 g (8 oz) unsalted butter, melted
half a 450 g (1 lb) jar apricot jam

Method

Start the custard by bringing the milk to the boil, then dissolving in it 6 tbsp of the vanilla sugar.* (If you do not have vanilla sugar to hand, use caster sugar with the addition of 2 tsp vanilla essence.) Set aside.

Whisk the egg yolks into the single cream with the citrus zest and the cognac, and add this mix to the boiled milk, whisking vigorously together.

Grease the inside of a large oval gratin dish (a cast-iron Le Creuset type is good) with a little of the butter and sprinkle half the raisins over the bottom. (This helps to create an easy way of lifting the portions out to serve.) Now cut the slices of bread into triangular quarters, and dip one side of the bread into the melted butter. Make a layer of triangles of buttered bread inside the dish, propping each one up against another so they are leaning slightly at an angle. (This will allow the custard mix to flow down between the layers and penetrate and cook evenly.) Now sprinkle the remaining raisins over the layer and arrange another layer of butter-dipped bread going the other way. Finish off with a third layer of bread, again arranged in the opposite direction. Pour the custard mix over slowly, ensuring that each top piece is soaked, and rest the pudding for 15 minutes to allow the fluid to settle and penetrate the whole dish.

Sprinkle over the remaining vanilla sugar and bake in a medium hot oven (180°C/350°F/Gas 4) for about 30 35 minutes. The position in the oven can be quite critical if you don't have a fan oven. The top of the pudding should be golden brown, with the bread quite crisp in parts. Conversely, the inner texture should be moist, soft and light, like a soufflé, but not runny. If in doubt, move the dish up or down accordingly. The second shelf down may be a good starting position.

Finally, when the pudding is taken out, brush the surface with warmed apricot jam to give it a good shine. This dessert can be served hot or even tepid, but loses its appeal when cooler. If you find you haven't had enough cholesterol, serve with clotted cream.

Baby spinach with smoked lardons, avocado and warm honey dressing

This, believe it or not, is fantastic! It can accompany many different dishes, or is perfect as a light summer supper meal. The secret is in the dressing – follow the directions very carefully or it might split.

*The Nosh Brothers' world-famous
warm honey dressing*
*2 large pinches sea salt ***
4 tbsp raspberry or cider vinegar
*4 tbsp clear honey (a strong one such as Greek
    Mountain or Australian is good)*
8 tbsp virgin olive oil
freshly ground black pepper

Salad
*450 g (1 lb) baby spinach leaves (de-stemmed
    weight)*
20 rashers smoked streaky bacon
2 tbsp olive oil
4 firm but ripe avocados

* Salt will not dissolve in oil, or honey, so ensure the salt is fully dissolved into the vinegar before adding the rest of the ingredients.

Dressing method

The proportions are: 1 of vinegar, 1 of honey, 2 of oil. For eight people you will need the above. Dissolve the salt in the vinegar, then stir in the honey, then add the oil and stir. Season with plenty of black pepper. You can warm the dressing up on a very low heat in a saucepan *very gently* – but don't overheat it, or it will split and the flavours will evaporate.

Salad method

Wash and drain the spinach. Discard any tough stems, damaged, bruised or discoloured leaves. Divide between individual plates.

Cut the bacon across the grain of the streaky layers in 5 mm (¼ in) wide strips, and fry in olive oil until crisp (alternatively, bake the pieces in the oven until crisp), then drain dry on kitchen paper.

Slice the avocados in half, de-stone them, and slice the flesh* into 5 mm (¼ in) thick slices. Fan out on the bed of spinach. Sprinkle crispy bacon generously over the top of the salad, and pour over the warm dressing. Serve immediately.

* *A little lemon or lime juice rubbed on to the avocado will prevent discoloration.*

MAIN COURSE 6

Roast fillet of pork with a mustard and macadamia nut crust

Suggested accompaniment
Dauphinoise potatoes (see page 144)
Sweet and sour red cabbage (see page 152)

This is a dish stolen from a dreadful man, so we won't give you his name (and save ourselves the libel suit), but he was really dreadful – trust us. However, it's a wonderful dish and easy to prepare.

> *4 fillets of pork (allow 225 g/8 oz untrimmed weight per person)*
> *sea salt and ground white pepper*
> *120 ml (4 fl oz) olive oil*
> *8 tbsp grainy Dijon mustard*
> *225 g (8 oz) shelled macadamia nuts, finely chopped*
> *2 large onions, peeled and finely chopped*
> *1 large wine glass white wine*
> *300 ml (½ pint) chicken stock (see page 155)*
> *1 medium can (14 oz / 250 g) apricots, drained and puréed*
> *freshly ground black pepper*

Method

Trim the fillets of all skin and sinews, and cut them 'square' so that each piece is a neat cylinder about 10 cm (4 in) in length. Reserve the trimmings.

Season the pork with salt and white pepper, and seal the meat all over in a hot, lightly oiled pan. Then, when cool enough to touch, roll one side of the meat cylinder in mustard and then into the chopped nuts, pressing down so that they stick. Set aside. Reserve any meat juices that gather.

To make the sauce, simply sauté the onions in 2 tbsp of the olive oil on a low heat until soft, then add the meat trimmings and fry until they are cooked through (about 5 minutes). Add the white wine and stock (including any reserved meat juices), and simmer for at least another 5–10 minutes, reducing the liquid by about two-thirds. Remove the meat trimmings using a slotted spoon, then add half the apricot purée to the remaining liquid and season to taste. The sauce should be a typical wine gravy with the slightly sweet taste of the apricots coming through. (Don't overdo the fruit, or the sauce will lose its savoury nature.)

The fillets should be roasted at a medium high heat (220°C/425°F/Gas 7) for about 12 minutes.* You can test the readiness of the meat by gently prodding the pork to check its degree of rareness (taking care not to burn yourself, or the nuts!). Serve with the meat nut-crust-side uppermost, on top of the sauce, with a fine grating of fresh black pepper.

* *Pork fillet is a very lean cut and should not be over-roasted. A degree of pinkness in the loin centre is ideal. Overcooking it will dry the meat out and render it tough.*

DESSERT 6

Pear tarte Tatin

Pear *tarte Tatin* is just great served with ice cream or clotted cream. It's easy to do, but remember not to take the pan out of the oven without a thick glove or the rest of the dinner will be held at Accident & Emergency (which can be slow unless you go private) so, poor people, watch out for delays in finishing dinner.

You will need a metal-handled cast-iron frying pan of about 23–25 cm (9–10 in) in diameter. It is unlikely you will have a large enough pan or stove to make an eight-portion tart, so you'll have to have *two* pans (or at least, make this dessert in two attempts).

2 × 225 g (8 oz) blocks fresh good-quality bought puff pastry
12 large firm under-ripe pears, peeled and cored, sliced into 5 mm (¼ in) thick slices (at widest point)

225 g (8 oz) caster sugar
120 ml (4 fl oz) water
110 g (4 oz) slightly salted butter, in small pieces

Method

Roll out the pastry blocks to a thickness of 5 mm (¼ in), and cut into two circles which are at least 2.5 cm (1 in) wider than the pan you will use. Chill in the freezer for at least 10 minutes.

In the clean heavy-based frying pan dissolve half the sugar in a quarter of the water over a low heat and then turn up the flame to high, adding the remaining quarter of the water when the sugar begins to turn to caramel (the sugar will start to turn browner with that distinctive toffee aroma). (Remember, don't overcook the sugar, otherwise it will turn blackish and bitter, in which case you will have to throw it away and start again!)

When nearly caramelized, add half the butter in small pieces. Stir it in, and then arrange half the slices of pear in the pan in a spiral, starting in the middle, overlapping them with the thick side uppermost. Continue to cook the fruit in the caramel, browning it on a high heat, for about 5–10 minutes until cooked but not mushy.

Take the pan off the heat and place a disc of pastry over the fruit. Carefully tuck the flap of spare pastry *under* the fruit. Place in a hot (200–220°C/375–400°F/Gas 5–6) oven for about 10–12 minutes until the pastry has risen and is baked golden-brown.

Remove the pan (taking care to use a thick heat-insulating cloth to protect your hands), and allow to rest for 1–2 minutes. Then loosen the edge of the pastry with a sharp knife. With a large retaining plate on top of the tart, upturn the pan (don't forget the cloth!) and allow the tart to flip over on to the plate so that the fruit is now visible as the top of the tart. The pears should have a brown coloration where they have been cooking in the sauce which should be sticky and cover the entire surface generously. Don't worry if any of the pears come unstuck on the pan – simply take them off with a palette knife and 'glue' them into place again.

Repeat this procedure with the remaining ingredients.

STARTER 7

Chilled vichyssoise with parsley pesto and garlic croutons

Vichyssoise is a very delicate tasting and filling soup that can be made more substantial by the addition of parsley pesto and some crisp croutons for texture.

Pesto
8 tbsp virgin olive oil
2 garlic cloves, peeled and chopped
a large handful of flat-leaf parsley leaves (no stems)
50 g (2 oz) pine nuts, toasted light brown
sea salt and freshly ground black pepper
4 heaped tbsp freshly grated Parmesan

Soup
50 g (2 oz) unsalted butter
450 g (1 lb) young leeks, whites only, cleaned and finely chopped

1 tbsp olive oil
3 shallots, peeled and finely diced
1 garlic clove, peeled and crushed
675 g (1½ lb) old floury potatoes, peeled and diced
1 tsp freshly grated nutmeg
salt and ground white pepper
1.2 litres (2 pints) chicken stock (see page 155)
300 ml (½ pint) whole milk

To serve
croutons *
150 ml (¼ pint) single cream

* Crush a few garlic cloves in olive oil and heat slowly for 5 minutes for the garlic essences to mingle with the oil. Do not let the garlic brown lest it impart a bitter taste to the oil. Then toss out the garlic, turn up the heat to medium and brown a few small cubes of white bread in the garlic oil until crisp. Drain well on kitchen paper.

Pesto method

You only need a small dollop of pesto to garnish each portion of soup, so small amounts can be made in advance as follows. Into a food processor put the first six ingredients, then blitz for 30 seconds or so until the garlic and parsley are well chopped. Then add the Parmesan, and blitz for a further 10 seconds. Spoon out into a ramekin dish and cover with clingfilm until needed. The flavours will improve over an hour or so, as the ingredients mingle.

Soup method

In a large saucepan, melt the butter in the oil and sweat off the leeks and shallots slowly over a low heat for 15 minutes until soft but not brown. Now add the garlic, potatoes, nutmeg, a small sprinkling of salt and white pepper and the stock, and bring to the boil. Turn down the heat and simmer for 30 minutes until the leek and potato are done, and then add the milk and process the soup through a blender. Then adjust the seasoning. Some people like to blitz this soup until it is a smooth blended purée, but we prefer it coarse and rustic in texture. Serve with a dollop of the parsley pesto, a few crisp croutons and a swirl of single cream.

MAIN COURSE 7

Mussels with shallots, white wine and herbs

Mussels are the most under-rated, inexpensive shellfish – and long may they remain so! Releasing copious amounts of liquid, they very kindly make their own sauce, and all we have to do is flavour it.

Mussels are filter feeders* and if kept cool they will keep their shells shut. If left to warm up out of the water their shells will open and that is where the possibility of contamination lies. Hence the old maxim: only eat mussels, oysters, etc. when there is an 'R' in the month, i.e. in cool weather. Sadly, due to intensive farming and an inclement environment, you rarely see mussels of any decent size these days.

> 6 tbsp olive oil
> 1 tbsp clarified butter
> 450 g (1 lb) shallots, peeled and finely diced
> 1 small red chilli, seeded and very finely chopped
> 6 garlic cloves, peeled and finely chopped
> 5.4 kg (12 lb) mussels,* scrubbed and de-bearded
> 300 ml (½ pint) white wine
> a handful of chopped herbs (parsley, basil, chervil, chives, etc.)
> freshly ground black pepper
> 8 tbsp single cream

*You can 'fatten up' your mussels on arrival simply by placing them in cold salt water (about four handfuls of salt per 9 litre/2 gallon bucket of cold fresh water) and stirring in oatmeal, previously blitzed in a blender on high speed for a few seconds, or some plain flour. If left for a few hours or even overnight the shellfish will filter feed, and this has the effect of allowing them to 'clean' themselves and fatten themselves up for cooking!

Method

The idea simply is to cook the shellfish in their own juices with the addition of simple flavourings as follows.

In a very large saucepan with a lid, heat the oil and butter and sauté the shallots, chilli and garlic for about 30 seconds over a medium heat. Then turn up the heat to high and toss in the mussels. (As the bulk of the shellfish are the shells themselves, you may have to prepare this dish in two parts and combine them later for serving.) Turn the mussels over so the unopened ones lie in the hot liquid and soon they will all open and release all their juices. Then add the wine and herbs and simmer for a few minutes, adding the black pepper and cream at the end. The rule is: if any shells do not open during cooking, then discard them; they are already dead and too risky to eat.

Serve with plenty of crusty bread to mop up the sauce, and provide your guests with side bowls for the empty shells.

Strawberry ice with tuile biscuits

This is a perfect recipe for fruits that may have gone too squishy for eating on their own and you don't know what to do with them. Slightly soggy fruits that have been packed too tightly in the punnet are perfect, but avoid any furry ones. These are obviously 'over' and will have a taint to them.

This ice cream has a very simple home-made feel to it. The fruit water in it forms slightly crunchy icy crystals and will scoop out better if the tub is left for 10 minutes to thaw slightly at room temperature.

*2 large punnets (or 4 small) of ripe English
    strawberries (about 450 g/1 lb)
about 1 teacup caster sugar (to taste) **
*1 teacup medium sherry (or ½ teacup kirsch)
600 ml (1 pint) double cream (extra thick dessert
    cream from Sainsbury's is good)*

* *Pale muscovado sugar tastes great in this recipe, but gives an unusual brownish tinge to the finished appearance that may not be appetizing.*

Method

Pick out any dodgy fruits, and rinse and hull the rest. In a mixing bowl stir the sugar into the sherry until dissolved, tip in the strawberries and mash with a potato masher until blended together. (You could use a blender or processor, but this manual method is good to give a coarse texture.) Whip the cream until just thickened (not too stiff – you don't want it to turn into butter), and fold in and mix thoroughly.

Pour into a plastic container with a lid, and freeze for 24 hours. There is *no need to stir at any time.*

Tuile biscuits

Tuiles are the 'Nancy-boy Potter' of the biscuit world, and what, you may ask, are they doing in a Nosh cookbook? Well, their reputation stems mostly from the fact that they're very fragile. Taste-wise and texture-wise they are real contenders, and knock brandy snaps into the end-of-the-pier bracket where they belong! (Note from Nick Nosh: *This recipe shouldn't be in the book at all – but I lost the argument!*)

These biscuits will absorb moisture and lose their crispness if made too far in advance – so make them on the day, an hour or two before the dinner.

*25 g (1 oz) plain flour
110 g (4 oz) ground almonds
110 g (4 oz) icing sugar
grated zest of 1 orange
juice of 5 oranges (about 275 ml/9 fl oz)
80 g (3 oz) unsalted butter, melted
butter for greasing*

Method

Tuiles are made by dropping biscuit mixture on to hot baking trays, where they will 'melt' and spread out before baking solid – so don't overcrowd your tray!

Combine the flour, almonds and sugar in a bowl with a spatula and stir in the zest and juice. Pour in the melted butter and mix thoroughly. Clingfilm the bowl and chill for a couple of hours.

Then a hot oven is required, 200°C/400°F/Gas 6.

Butter the trays generously – use baking parchment if you are worried about getting the biscuits out without chipping them. Using a dessertspoon, dipped in cold water, spoon out small mounds of paste, pressing down on each one with a palette knife dipped in cold water to make a flat cake about 6–7 cm (1½–2¼ in) across. Repeat to make about twenty biscuits. As with pancakes, the first biscuit will probably be a disaster, but once the tray heats up you'll get into your stride.

Bake each tray in the preheated oven for about 4–5 minutes or until golden brown, then remove from the oven. After resting to cool for 20 seconds, roll half the biscuits up lightly into a scroll (keep some in their original 'fan' shape), and let them cool fully for a couple of minutes. Don't burn your fingers, but remember, once fully cooled, you can't change their shape – they'll be too fragile and will crumble.

STARTER 8

Crostini with roasted red peppers and basil

Crostini are oven-toasted breads which are brushed with fine olive oil and make good bases for a variety of Italian toppings. Here we choose a version, which although vegetarian (God help us all) is nevertheless very flavoursome.

This starter is useful in that it can be served easily by hand if guests are standing, and if there are late arrivals you can hand them around like canapés.

4 large or 6 small red peppers
basic olive oil
150 ml (¼ pint) cold-pressed extra-virgin olive oil
2 garlic cloves, peeled and chopped

1 small bunch fresh basil
sea salt and freshly ground black pepper
1 large loaf ciabatta bread, sliced

Method

Coat each red pepper lightly using up about 3 tablespoons basic olive oil, and place on a foil-covered roasting tray in a very hot oven (240°C/475°F/Gas 9) for about 8 minutes, turning them over at least once to ensure even roasting. We have a gas barbecue in the garden which has a kettle-type lid and it is perfect for quickly heating to roasting temperature – and you can watch the progress of the peppers so much more easily. The skin of the peppers should be slightly charred and bubbling. This makes it easy to separate the skin from the flesh.

When done, remove to a cool high-sided tray and place the peppers, layering evenly if you have to, with clingfilm tightly over the top of the tray. They will cool slowly, condensing moisture on the inside of the clingfilm. When cool, you'll find they'll peel easily. (Don't overdo them in the oven otherwise the flesh will roast too hot and you'll end up with a very mushy result.)

When cooled, drained, cored, de-seeded and skinned, you can mix the peppers with a little extra-virgin oil, the garlic, some shredded basil and seasonings. Turn the peppers over by hand gently, so as not to break them up, and let them rest for the flavours to amalgamate.

To make the crostini, brush the top side of each ciabatta slice with olive oil and bake in a hot oven (220°C/425°F/Gas 7) for a few minutes until golden-brown. Then place some peppers on top, decorate with some fresh shredded basil leaves and serve.

Risotto of squids in their ink

Risotto of squids in their ink is fun – especially good if you have squeamish guests you wish to wind up. It tastes fab, but don't overcook the rice; it should have bite. Prepare your guests for black teeth afterwards. You've been warned!!

As risotto needs constant attention and stirring, it is advisable to make the squid part of the dish first and complete the rice part last. Risotto does need accurate timing. A few minutes too much and it is mushy; too little time, and it is gritty and inedible. Most arborio rice (depending on type and size of grain) needs about 18–20 minutes.

4 small squids
6 tbsp good-quality olive oil
a handful of fresh chopped parsley
1 large wine glass white wine
2 Spanish onions, peeled and diced
500 g (18 oz) arborio (risotto) rice
2 garlic cloves, peeled and chopped
1.2 litres (2 pints) fish stock (page 154)
*6 small sachets concentrated squid ink ***
sea salt and freshly ground black pepper
50 g (2 oz) Parmesan, finely grated

*** These can be bought relatively easily from good fishmongers.**

Squid method

Firstly, take off the outer purply-pink 'skin' of the squids and discard it. Now gut the squids. Cut off the heads above the eyes and retain the tentacles. Slice the squid thinly across the width of the body, and sauté it lightly in a little of the olive oil, adding some chopped parsley and a dash of the white wine, agitating the pan gently to form an 'emulsion' of the wine and oil, season and then set aside. (Do not overcook as you will warm the squids through for a few moments later to serve.)

Risotto method

In a large pan with a heavy base, sauté the onions with the rice in the olive oil on a medium heat for about 3 minutes, stirring and turning the rice over so that it is completely sealed and goes transparent. Add the garlic, remaining white wine and 600 ml (1 pint) fish stock. Bring to the boil and turn down the heat immediately on to very low to simmer the rice. Cooking a large amount of risotto is quite tricky as you'll need to turn the rice over often, as the bottom layer will naturally tend to cook before the top. So constant stirring is called for. As the rice absorbs the wine and stock, add more, a little at a time, in order not to cool down the bulk too much. You could also warm the stock a little first. Ideally risotto should be moist and yet not runny, al dente to the bite, yet not 'raw'.

After 12 minutes or so add more stock (as necessary, to keep the mixture moist and avoid any sticking to the pan base), as well as the contents of the sachets of ink. Stir in well. Naturally, the rice turns jet black at this stage. Then season and add the grated cheese, continuing to stir.

When the rice is cooked to perfection take off the heat. Remember, even spooning it on a hot plate, it will continue to cook on, rather like pasta, and will thicken and solidify, so keep adding dashes of stock right up to the end.

Serve the risotto with a generous spoonful of warmed squids and sauce over the top.

DESSERT 8

Peaches in dessert wine

An easy light dessert, this, after a substantial main course.

> 8 large ripe firm peaches, skin on
> 4 tbsp caster sugar
> ½ bottle Sauternes-type sweet dessert white wine
> 2 vanilla pods
>
> **To serve**
> double cream

Method

Stone the peaches, cutting each into two neat halves.

Make a syrup by dissolving the sugar in a couple of dashes of the wine and almost caramelizing it on a high heat (about 4 minutes or so). You want to colour up the sugar so it's very nearly the strong brown syrup we remember from the *tartes Tatin* (page 39) – but not quite. When the sugar starts to brown and give a distinctive caramel aroma, add the rest of the wine and the vanilla pods with the fruit, and reduce on a slow to medium simmer until the wine has become viscous and will coat the peaches.

Don't overcook the fruit or you'll get jam! The peaches should be firmish-to-soft without being mushy, and the syrup thick enough to coat the back of a spoon. Some double cream will accompany this dessert well.

STARTER 9

Smoked chicken salad with moon-dried tomatoes

Using plum tomatoes and following our recipe on page 148 you can keep the tomatoes in plain, herb or garlic oil for weeks and use them on salads and pastas to great effect. When smoked using our smoking method, the chicken becomes a truly wonderful dish. Hot-smoking the chicken can be easily done at home in the oven, you don't need special equipment, but beware of burning charcoal indoors: it is not safe without adequate ventilation or you'll die of fumes. Don't say we didn't warn you.

> 3 tbsp olive oil
> 3 large (225 g / 8 oz) skinless chicken breasts at
>   room temperature
> 2 tsp Cajun mixed spice *
> 1 bunch spring onions, trimmed
> mixed salad leaves (crisp ones are best here, such
>   as cos etc., and even some proportion of
>   iceberg is acceptable **)
> vinaigrette for dressing (see page 154)
> 12 moon-dried tomatoes
> sea salt

* *Anglicized versions of Cajun spice abound in supermarkets and try hard to be 'the real thing'. They often have exotic-sounding names, but try to get hold of the American genuine article.*

** Iceberg is not one of our favourites generally, but here, as with some Mexican recipes, its watery, crunchy texture goes well with the chicken.*

For the smoking you will need a small metal or foil tray, a large metal tray with high sides, and charcoal/woodchips. Exotic woodchips like mesquite and maple are great but can be hard to get in the UK. Most good garages and supermarkets stock oak and sometimes hickory, if you're lucky.

Method

Brush oil over the chicken breasts and season lightly with the Cajun spice to give a piquant flavour. But don't overdo it, the spice should not mask the smoky element.

The idea is to heat some charcoal by placing it in the small metal tray over a hot flame until combusting. Then sprinkle over some damp woodchips (previously soaked in water) to create the smoke. Place this in the large tray in the bottom of a medium hot oven (180°C/350°F/Gas 4) with a wire rack of chicken breasts arranged above it, and cover the whole lot with a foil lid to hold the smoke in (punched with a couple of slits for venting). The chicken can then be hot-smoked for about 15–25 minutes. (Ensure that the kitchen is well ventilated, as charcoal issues carbon monoxide fumes that should not be inhaled.) Ensure too that the small charcoal dish is at one side of the large tray, otherwise when cooking the chicken will drip on to the hot coals and extinguish them.

The chicken should have a moist interior that, although wet-looking when sliced through, should not actually be pink.

Mix the spring onions with the salad leaves, and dress with vinaigrette to taste. Divide between individual plates, and scatter chopped moon-dried tomatoes on top. Thinly slice the chicken breasts at a slant, arrange over the tomatoes and season.

Bavette of beef with braised potato and onion in beer

Bavette is basically a French name for the long triangular piece of hindquarter beef skirt (the diaphragm-type muscle that forms the boundaries of the offal cavity), a cut which is much underrated, and which isn't expensive. (The 'flatter' forequarter piece of skirt is known as the *onglet.*) The only problem is that *bavette* can only be cooked rare to medium rare; once you stray into the realms of medium, the flesh toughens and renders it useless – so be warned! Timing is crucial.

You will need a metal-handled frying pan.

Potato and onion
1.4 kg (3 lb) old potatoes, scrubbed
sea salt
675 g (1½ lb) onions, peeled and sliced into thin
    rounds
3 garlic cloves, peeled and crushed
3 tbsp olive oil
25 g (1 oz) unsalted butter
a large pinch of freshly grated nutmeg
ground white pepper
600 ml (1 pint) robust bitter or pale or brown
    ale
25 g (1 oz) butter, melted, to finish
freshly ground black pepper

Beef
1.8 kg (4 lb) beef skirt (ask your butcher for
    bavette, *see above*)

4 tbsp olive oil
sea salt and ground white pepper
2 tbsp Dijon mustard
1 wine glass red wine for deglazing

Potato method

Parboil the potatoes in their skins in salted water until half cooked. Refresh in cold water to allow easy peeling, then slice into 3 mm (⅛ in) thick discs. Sauté the onion and garlic in the oil and butter over a medium heat until softened and then spread half this mixture on the bottom of an oiled baking or gratin dish. Then arrange alternative layers of potato and onion, seasoning each layer with salt, white pepper and nutmeg, finishing with potato. The final layer should be about 2 cm (1½–1¾ in) high. Pour over the beer and cover the tray with foil.

Bake in a medium hot oven (180°C/350°F/Gas 4) for 1 hour and then remove the foil cover. Brush the surface generously with the melted butter, sprinkle with black pepper and cook on, uncovered, for 15 minutes at the top of the oven, until golden-brown in colour.

When the potatoes are done (test by pushing in a skewer if in doubt) start to cook the beef. It will not take long.

Beef method

Preheat the oven to 230°C/450°F/Gas 8.

Prepare the beef by trimming into eight portions, oiling it lightly and seasoning with salt and white pepper. Cover the pieces lightly with the Dijon mustard. Allow to rest and come to room temperature while the potatoes are cooking.

Heat a metal-handled frying pan to hot and then pour in the olive oil. You may have to do the meat in two batches, otherwise the pan will be overcrowded. The beef is very lean and should be sealed with the juices inside. The best way is to seal the meat on all sides in the pan until some colour is taken on, and then put the pan straight into the hot oven for 4 minutes or so. You can test the meat by prodding it with a forefinger quickly to assess the rareness. (Don't forget a cloth around the hot handle!) There should be a distinct 'give' in the meat. When done, deglaze the pan with a dash of red wine.

To serve

To serve, the skirt should be carved at a 45 degree angle against the grain in thin slices and placed on a bed of the braised potato with the pan juices poured over the top.

DESSERT 9

Crème caramel with Stroh rum

You will need ramekin dishes for this dessert. If you are making eight portions, it is advisable to make an extra one, to test the mixture near the end of the cooking time. You then don't spoil the main batch for the meal. Stroh rum is the brand name of a mighty Austrian rum, popular with après-skiers. It has a distinctive caramel flavour that lends itself so well to this dessert. If you can't get any Stroh, use a good quality dark rum from the West Indies.

1.2 litres (2 pints) whole milk
4 eggs
5 egg yolks
3 tbsp vanilla sugar (see page 152) or 2 tsp vanilla essence
2 tbsp Stroh or dark rum (see above)
light sunflower oil

Caramel
225 g (8 oz) caster sugar
about 150 ml (¼ pint) water
4 tbsp Stroh or dark rum

Method

Scald the milk, that is, bring the milk slowly up to boiling point, and then quickly remove it from the heat. Break the eggs into a round-bottomed bowl, then add the extra yolks. Whisk lightly with a balloon whisk until creamy but not frothy. Whisk in the vanilla sugar, rum and milk and set aside at room temperature.

Prepare the caramel by dissolving the sugar over a gentle heat with the water, then boil rapidly without stirring until a rich brown colour, taking care not to overcook the caramel and render it bitter and unusable. You can 'stop' the caramel when ready by placing the hot saucepan bottom into a tray of cold water. Add the rum and dissolve well into the caramel.

Grease small ramekin dishes on bottom and sides with a little light sunflower oil, then coat with the syrupy caramel, ensuring there is a generous amount in the bottom of each dish. Strain the custard mixture through a fine sieve (or clean muslin) to remove any egg 'threads', and then pour into each ramekin to about 1 cm (½ in) from the top. Cover each ramekin with a small square of kitchen foil, pulled tight across to 'seal' the top. Place the dishes in a bain-marie tray of hot water, and then into a medium oven (160°C/325°F/Gas 3) for about 30–40 minutes until just set. Remove the ramekins from the oven and rest in a cool place. (The latent heat in each dish will continue to cook the custard mix, so use your spare dish to test and try the state of the custard by prodding the surface and then digging the spoon right in and testing it direct.) If the custards are still very runny, replace lid(s) and continue to bake in the bain-marie tray for another 5 minutes, then test again. Leave to become cold before serving.

STARTER 10

Greek salad of home-made feta cheese, tomato, cucumber and Kalamata olives

With this menu you need a light starter, as the second course is so filling (and the dessert is no lighter). Feta and olive salads are a pivot of the Greek kitchen, as everyone who has visited the Greek islands knows. Made from sheep's milk or goats' milk, fresh feta cheese is simple to make at home. You can buy fresh goats' or sheep's milk in supermarkets nowadays, but cows' milk makes a reasonably good substitute. Get good tomatoes – they make a big difference to the overall effect of this classic Greek dish.

2.3 litres (4 pints) cows', goats' or sheep's milk
1 tbsp vegetarian rennet or 120 ml (4 fl oz) white
  vinegar
2 tsp fine sea salt

Salad
1 cucumber, peeled and finely sliced
450 g (1 lb) plum tomatoes, sliced

110 g (4oz) Kalamata olives
lemon dressing *
2 medium red onions, finely chopped
2 tsp dried oregano

* Use the basic dressing recipe on page 154, but replace the vinegar with lemon juice.

Method

Cheese is simply the 'curds' (solids) separated from the 'whey'. This separation can be easily achieved by the adding of rennet to curdle milk, but it can also be done using 120 ml (4 fl oz) white vinegar.

Bring the milk to the boil and let it cool to lukewarm. Add rennet or vinegar and stir around to separate the curds. When the curds have solidified, strain the liquid off through a sieve. Then sprinkle fine salt into the curds (1 tsp per 225 g/8 oz curds) and mix thoroughly. When the curds have fully drained, place them in a clean muslin cloth, folded to contain all the cheese, and squeeze it flat on a draining board with a heavy weight on top to flatten the cheese (a cast-iron saucepan is fine). The cheese should flatten to a thickness of about 1–2.5 cm (½–1 in), and the juices will be 'pressed out' with the help of the salt.

When the cheese has dried out sufficiently (about 2 hours should be enough), cut it into small cubes and place it on a bed of cucumber and tomato slices, sprinkled with Kalamata olives, and dressed with lemon dressing. The addition of some red onions and a sprinkle of dried oregano gives a strong bite.

Any cheese left over can be kept for a week or two preserved in olive oil.

Roast belly of pork with caramelized apple, parsnips and bubble and squeak

A useful recipe this, as it is a roast you can partly pre-cook to save time, thus allowing more time for the cook to socialize! Most people think belly of pork is a fatty dish: it can be if you don't cook it correctly, but cooked properly, the crackling is fantastic.

40 cm (16 in) long piece of lean pork belly
sea salt and freshly ground black pepper
juice of 1 lemon
900 g (2 lb) parsnips
6 large firm dessert apples (e.g. Braeburn)
2 tbsp olive oil
50 g (2 oz) unsalted butter
4 tbsp caster sugar

Bubble and squeak
900 g (2 lb) mashed potato (see page 147, no milk, butter or cream used in preparation)
1 small Savoy cabbage, de-stemmed and chopped
2 shallots, peeled and chopped
3 rashers smoked streaky bacon, chopped into small lardons
50 g (2 oz) unsalted butter
salt and freshly ground black pepper
1 egg
plain flour for dusting
2 tbsp olive oil

Pork method 1

Firstly, trim the pork of all visible bones, and score the skin deeply and finely with 3 mm (⅛ in) wide cuts to create the crackling. Season the crackling and underside well with salt and pepper, and sprinkle with the juice of the lemon (this will help the crackling become crispy). Every 5 cm (2 in) score the skin particularly deeply – this will denote the final portion size: 5 cm (2 in) width per person.

Pre-roast the joint slowly in a roasting tin at a medium heat (160°C/325°F/Gas 3) under foil for about 50–60 minutes or until the crackling starts to become crisp and bubbles. Pre-roasting at a medium heat will also help the middle part of the belly to soften and reduce the fatty layers, which will drain out into the pan. (This can be kept as dripping for future cooking, although the modern vogue for less fat will probably consign dripping to a vague memory for the over-40s!)

Bubble and squeak method

The bubble and squeak is simply made by blanching the cabbage for 4 minutes, then draining and adding it to the mashed potato in a ratio of 2 parts potato to 1 part cabbage. Cook the shallots along with the lardons in the butter until softened. Add to the cabbage mix. Season, then add the egg to bind.* Shape into round patties on a wooden board and dust lightly with flour to stop them sticking. Store at room temperature until ready for frying.

* It is important not to be tempted to add any rich additions at this stage as the mixture will end up too sloppy for making good firm patties. The cabbage and shallots also release a little liquid during cooking.

Vegetable method

Prepare the vegetables by peeling and quartering the parsnips, and coring and slicing the apples into rounds, retaining the skin. Parboil the parsnips for 2–3 minutes. When drained and cooled, fry the parsnips and apple rings quickly in the oil and butter. Sprinkle with the sugar, then turn the vegetables over on a high heat for a few minutes until they start to caramelize and are coated with a sticky brown residue of sugar. Do not overcook at this stage – they need to retain their shape during the last roasting stage with the pork.

Pork method 2

Finally, when required, you can roast the pork quickly at a high heat (220–230°C/425–450°F/Gas 7–8) for 15–20 minutes to heat up the meat, crisp the crackling and roast the vegetables to a rich golden-brown colour. While the joint is roasting you can finally fry the bubble and squeak patties in the olive oil in a medium hot frying pan until they, too, get a brownish crisp coat.

The pork should carve itself naturally along the deep lines scored previously and, if pre-roasted well, should not really be a particularly fatty dish.

DESSERT 10

Chocolate mousse with Cointreau

300 g (10 oz) luxury dark Continental chocolate
   (75% cocoa solids)
3 egg yolks, at room temperature
7 egg whites, at room temperature *
4 tbsp caster sugar

a large dash of Cointreau
50 g (2 oz) unsalted butter, softened

⁎ *Take care not to allow even the tiniest bit of yolk to enter the whites, otherwise they will not stiffen on whisking.*

Method

Break the chocolate into little squares and place in a bowl over some hot water to melt them. Do not over-heat or you'll coagulate the chocolate. Whisk half the sugar with the egg yolks until smooth and creamy. Then, with a clean dry whisk, whisk the whites until stiff and foamy and then add the remaining sugar and continue to whisk together. The secret here is to add the sugar towards the end, otherwise, if added too early, the whites will not stiffen into peaks. On the addition of the sugar the peaks will take on a glossy look and you should then add the Cointreau. Then divide the egg whites between three separate dishes.

Add the butter to the melted chocolate and remove the pan from the heat. Now the timing is crucial. Once 'cool' materials are added to the chocolate mix the mousse will start to solidify, so rapid whisking is required.

First, fold the yolk mix into the first lot of whites and mix thoroughly but gently. Then add the chocolate mix quickly and fold thoroughly together to blend the chocolate without any 'chips' appearing.

Next, fold in the second batch of whites gently with a large spoon to give volume, and stir around. Then add the final batch, folding very gently to distribute the whites evenly and keep the mousse as light as possible. Work lightly with upward movements to get as much air as possible into the bowl, and don't overwork each stage. Stop as soon as the whites are fully incorporated.

Pour the mousse mixture neatly and quickly into a serving bowl, or individual ramekins or dessert glasses, and refrigerate for a couple of hours before serving. This is such a 'full-on' recipe for mousse that you can pour it into egg cups and you will be sur-prised how filling it still is! Remove the mousse from the fridge 15 minutes or so before serving – it's best chilled but not so cold as to kill the flavour!

Menus for the Well Off

Introduction

We have expanded this section to bring you sixteen menus instead of the ten or so in each of the other sections. We imagine, realistically, that the bulk of the entertaining requirement will be fulfilled by this. We don't know about you, but the Noshes prefer people to entertain extremely well on a regular basis rather than royally, only occasionally.

The menus here include some ingredients that you'll maybe need a specialist supplier of, say egg Marsala or truffle oil. But we have tried to keep within the boundaries of good-quality supermarkets. A few years ago, it was almost impossible to get items like quail or pheasant down your local high street. Now they come stuffed or with two different herb marinades.

The combinations of recipes are put together as a guide only. Some of the items may be seasonal and temporarily unavailable. In this case, use your imagination to substitute other ingredients or dishes of a similar nature, and whenever possible try to obtain the best possible quality. Wild salmon is not always in season, but compared with farmed it has incomparable taste. It goes without saying that free-range birds will have none of that insipid watery flesh that battery-reared ones have. So go for the best.

If you have difficulty in finding any quality ingredients you can enquire about sourcing them at Food from Britain in London. This organization exists primarily to help exporters to get fine foods to their potential markets, but in our experience, the consumer must demand the best available . . . and we have always found them very helpful. So give them a ring.

Menu 11

Crab cakes with red pepper mayonnaise

Osso bucco with smoked tomato risotto

Lemon tart

Menu 12

Artichokes with a creamed garlic dressing

Marinated seared fillets of salmon with ginger

Fresh strawberries with lemon juice and black pepper

Menu 13

Fish soup with rouille toasts

Roast glazed spiced gammon

American breakfast cake

Menu 14

Singapore laksa

Chicken satay with cucumber, red rice and gado gado salad

Jackfruit fritters

Menu 15

Bruschetta with marinated grilled squid and a green salsa

Grilled rump of lamb with button onions

Crème brûlée with candied ginger and Stroh rum

Menu 16

Rocket salad with pan-fried duck, poached egg and truffle oil

Pot-roast beef with field mushrooms and red wine

Armagnac and prune tart

Menu 17

Ceviche of monkfish with chillies and orange

*Grilled red snapper fillets and prawns with
tequila mayonnaise*

Apple layer pudding

Menu 18

Stracciatella Romana *with egg and lemon*

Pork Milanese with linguine, peppers and courgettes

Giant strawberries dipped in Belgian chocolate

Menu 19

Spicy mushroom (yam het) *salad*

*Roast breast of duck on pak choy and beansprouts
with soy and ginger*

*Rujak (Balinese spiced fruits) with coconut rum
custard*

Menu 20

Gazpacho

Duck confit *on stir-fried spinach with chanterelles*

Fresh date tart with Cointreau

Menu 21

*Chicory salad with Gorgonzola, walnuts and
orange vinaigrette*

*Salmon in spinach leaf parcels with sorrel
mayonnaise and wild rice with toasted almonds*

Banana toffee pie

Menu 22

Capellini with wild mushrooms and truffle oil

Chicken Valdostana

Tiramisu 'espresso forte' (2 versions!)

Menu 23

Tuscan bean soup

Roast leg of lamb with anchovies

Raspberry ice cream

Menu 24

Spiced peppers on butter-rich cornbread

*Southern chicken with Plantation pot salad and
Nosh potato salad*

Pecan and apricot cookies

Menu 25

Confit *of duck livers on cabbage ragout*

*Brochettes of monkfish, pancetta and rosemary with
avocado couscous*

Hot chocolate pie

Menu 26

*Asparagus with shaved Parmesan and extra-virgin
olive oil*

Calves' liver Veneziana on saffron risotto

Raspberry and pecan zuppa inglese

Crab cakes with red pepper mayonnaise

Seasonings
½ *tsp each of grated nutmeg, mustard powder and*
ground black pepper
1 *tsp each of paprika, onion powder and sea salt*
1 *tsp each of freshly chopped garlic, parsley and*
coriander
2 *tsp freshly chopped chives*

Crab cakes
1 *large egg*
3 *tbsp double cream*
150 *g (5 oz) finely grated parboiled potato*
1 *large mild onion, peeled and finely grated*
4 *tbsp plain flour*
550 *g (1¼ lb) mixed crabmeat, white and dark*
meat
vegetable oil ∗

Red pepper mayonnaise
300 *ml (½ pint) thick mayonnaise (see page 153)*
1 *red pepper, cored, seeded, chopped and*
drained
juice of ½ lemon

∗ *Use enough oil in the pan to fry at least the bottom*
half of the fishcake. Corn or sunflower oil (or indeed,
any good light oil) is good – but not soya oil which is
inferior and gives a rank flavour and aroma.

Method

Combine the seasonings, egg and cream in a processor and blend for 15 seconds on a medium speed or
pulse.

Combine the potato, onion, flour and the egg mixture in a large bowl and mix thoroughly with a spoon. Add the crabmeat gently, folding it carefully so as not to break up the meat too much. Form the mixture into patties that can be flattened while in the pan.

Heat a little oil in a proved cast-iron or non-stick pan (heavy-bottomed is best), and shallow-fry the patties in small batches. Cook for about 5–6 minutes turning frequently (don't crowd the pan).

When golden-brown, remove, drain on kitchen paper and keep warm.

Ensure the oil remaining in the pan is allowed to get back to a decent heat before doing the rest, otherwise the cakes will absorb the oil without cooking crisply and the centre of the patties will be soggy.

To make the red pepper mayonnaise, whizz up all the ingredients in a processor until the mixture is creamy red in colour. Serve on the side as a dipping sauce.

MAIN COURSE 11

Osso bucco with smoked tomato risotto

Osso bucco is a stew of the hind shin of a milk-fed veal calf cut across the grain of the meat. Ideally, the pieces of meat are 10–11 cm (3½–4 in) diameter sections about 5–6 cm (1½ in) thick. Inside the circle of meat is the round bone and inside this, the marrow, which is the essence of the dish. Purists argue incessantly whether tomatoes are traditional in *ossobuco alla Milanese*. We have taken a midway course here by including a small amount of toma-

toes in the stew with some smoked tomatoes* in the accompanying risotto.

* *The method for oven smoking can be found earlier on page 47. Simply replace the chicken with tomatoes and then place them in the oven following the moon-dried process on page 148.*

> *80 g (3 oz) unsalted butter*
> *3 tbsp olive oil*
> *2 Spanish onions, peeled and finely chopped*
> *1 large carrot, finely chopped*
> *1 large celery stalk plus leaves, peeled of stringy bits and chopped*
> *1 garlic clove, peeled and crushed*
> *8 osso bucci (see above)*
> *6 tbsp plain flour*
> *sea salt and freshly ground black pepper*
> *250 ml (8 fl oz) dry white wine*
> *225 g (8 oz) canned plum tomatoes*
> *600 ml (1 pint) veal stock (see page 155)*
> *1 tsp caster sugar*
> *1 tsp chopped fresh thyme*
>
> *To serve*
> *gremolata (see page 21)*

Osso bucco method

Heat a heavy-based sauté pan, add the butter and half the oil, and sweat the onion, carrot, celery and garlic for 8 minutes, stirring occasionally.

Coat the veal pieces in seasoned flour, shaking off any excess, and fry the veal to seal it in the remaining olive oil. Brown well on all sides. Deglaze with the wine and add the tomatoes, stock, sugar and thyme. Transfer to a casserole with a tight-fitting lid and cook over a very low heat for 1½–2 hours. During cooking baste the veal occasionally and add more stock if it looks too dry. You should aim to cook the veal to perfectly soft throughout, but do not allow the meat to fall off the bone. If, on the other hand, the sauce looks too thin, decant most of it and boil it rapidly to reduce it to a thick glaze. Serve the osso bucci on top of the risotto with a sprinkling of gremolata.

Smoked tomato risotto

2 Spanish onions, peeled and diced
500 g (18 oz) arborio (risotto) rice
6 tbsp olive oil
2 garlic cloves, peeled and chopped
1 large wine glass white wine
1.2 litres (2 pints) chicken stock (see page 155)
12 smoked dried tomatoes (see pages 47 and 148)
    chopped
50 g (2 oz) Parmesan, finely grated
sea salt and freshly ground black pepper

Method

As risotto needs constant attention and stirring, it is advisable to make the osso bucco part of the dish first and complete this part last.

In a large pan with a heavy base, sauté the onions with the rice in the olive oil on a medium heat for about 3 minutes, stirring and turning the rice over so that it is completely sealed and goes transparent. Add the garlic, white wine and 600 ml (1 pint) of the stock. Bring to the boil, add the smoked tomatoes, and turn down the heat immediately to very low to simmer the rice, stirring constantly. As the rice absorbs the wine and stock, add more, a little at a time, in order not to cool down the bulk too much. Ideally risotto should be moist and yet not runny, al dente to the bite, yet not 'raw'.

After 12 minutes or so, add the Parmesan and more stock, as necessary, to keep the mixture moist and avoid any sticking to the pan base. Then season, continuing to stir until cooked to perfection.

Lemon tart

Sablé pastry is essentially a shortbread dough which, although very fragile, has a beautiful texture and an incomparable taste.

Traditionally, this tart is served cool, but beware, the pastry will get soggy if kept chilled in a fridge. Store it in a cool place.

Sablé *pastry*
300 g (10 oz) plain flour
110 g (4 oz) icing sugar
25 g (1 oz) ground almonds
175 g (6 oz) unsalted butter, softened and
    diced
2 egg yolks
a pinch of sea salt
a couple of drops of vanilla essence
plain flour for dusting
eggwash (1 yolk plus 1 tbsp whole milk)

Filling
10 medium eggs
400 g (14 oz) caster sugar
zest and juice of 5 lemons (unwaxed)
350 ml (12 fl oz) fresh double cream

To serve
icing sugar
clotted cream

Pastry method

Sift the flour, sugar and almonds together onto a board or clean smooth worktop, and make a well in the centre. Put the cubes of butter into the well with the egg yolks and work together with your hands.

Add the salt and vanilla, and mix the pastry well together into a smooth-textured ball. Wrap in a polythene bag and chill in the fridge for 1 hour. Do not overwork the dough, otherwise it will become stiff and difficult to work with.

Preheat the oven to 200°C/400°F/Gas 6.

Roll out the pastry on a well-floured board to a thickness of 3 cm (1¼ in). Grease and flour a 25 cm (10 in) diameter flan tin. Place the pastry carefully in the tin, and trim the top edge to leave about 5 mm (¼ in) above the top of the flan tin top. Chill in the fridge for about 30 minutes (this will stop the pastry collapsing during the first 5 minutes in the oven). Bake blind in the oven (lined carefully with silicone baking parchment and baking beans) for 15 minutes, then remove from the oven, take off the paper and bean filling, and eggwash the interior. This will seal the pastry against cracks and any filling leaking out. Now return to the oven at the slightly lower temperature of 150–160°C/300–325°F/Gas 2–3 for another 5 minutes until the glaze is slightly golden-brown.

Filling method

Break the eggs into a bowl with the sugar and blend until smooth. Next, add the lemon zest and the juice. Whisk the cream lightly until slightly thickened, with a homogenized texture, and add to the eggs. Stir all together and pour into the finished flan case. Bake in the oven (still set at 150–160°C/300–325°F/Gas 2–3) for about 1–1¼ hours until the filling has set. When ready, take out of the oven. Remove the outer ring, and slide a palette knife gently under to release the tart from the metal base. *Sablé* pastry is very fragile so take great care.

To serve

Sprinkle the top of the tart with icing sugar. Serve with clotted cream if desired.

Artichokes with a creamed garlic dressing

1 large artichoke per person
sea salt and freshly ground black pepper
3 tbsp plain flour
juice of 1 lemon, squeezed halves retained
3 garlic cloves, peeled and crushed
2 tbsp mayonnaise (see page 153)
175 ml (6 fl oz) vinaigrette (see page 154)

Method

Cut the artichoke stems off close to the base of each head and, with kitchen scissors, trim the tips of the bottom few rows of leaves, leaving any softer smaller leaves intact.

Place the trimmed artichokes into boiling, well-salted water along with the flour, the lemon juice and squeezed peel.* Bring it back to the boil and simmer for about 30 minutes until the artichoke base is soft when pricked with a skewer. Naturally, this time will vary, depending on the size of artichoke you are cooking. You should be able to pull off an inner leaf (not an outer one) when the flesh is cooked enough. When cool enough to handle, scoop out the hairy inner choke with a teaspoon and discard it. Season with salt and black pepper.

For the garlic dressing, simply whisk the garlic and mayonnaise into the vinaigrette to form a creamy dressing that's the perfect alternative to the traditional clarified butter. Serve each artichoke with a small pot of dressing to dip leaves and flesh into.

The lemon will prevent discoloration of the artichoke flesh, and the flour will hold the bulbs in suspension within the water – so they do not bob up above the water surface.

MAIN COURSE 12

Marinated seared fillets of salmon with ginger

Suggested accompaniment
Sugar-snap peas and Jersey Royals (see page 151)

Use wild salmon if in season. They benefit from having a flavour that comes from a wild diet of crustacea and not just 'pellets'. The wild salmon's flesh is also less fatty than the farmed type, and will take on the ginger seasoning magnificently.

1 × 5 cm (2 in) piece of root ginger, peeled and grated
6 spring onions, finely chopped
2 large wine glasses white wine
juice of 2 limes
8 × 225 g (8 oz) salmon fillets, boned and skinned
sea salt and ground white pepper
3 tbsp olive oil
unsalted butter for greasing
freshly ground black pepper

Method

Put the ginger and spring onion into a suitable dish. Pour over the wine and lime juice, and marinate the salmon fillets in the liquid for 1 hour.

Preheat the oven to 230°C/450°F/Gas 8.

Drain and season the fillets, reserving the marinade, and preheat the frying pan (a black mild steel pan, seasoned and heated to hot temperature, is ideal). Sear the fillets in the pan in hot olive oil to seal the flesh on both sides. Place them on a buttered baking tray to finish off in the oven. Before placing the fish fillets in the oven, pour the marinade over them. Four to five minutes in the oven should be enough for a rare centre – lengthen the time by 1 minute or so if you require a more medium centre to your fish. Serve with the pan juices poured back over the fillets, and sprinkled with black pepper.

DESSERT 12

Fresh strawberries with lemon juice and black pepper

175 g (6 oz) strawberries per person, hulled
juice of 4 lemons
freshly ground black pepper

Method

There's nothing to beat English strawberries at their peak. Unfortunately, many fruits available all year round may look OK, but their forced growth in hothouses leaves much to be desired in the way of flavour.

In Mick's grandmother's day all that was permissible was a sprinkling of caster sugar, and sometimes kirsch. Other people favour balsamic vinegar and obscure liqueurs, but a surprise Nosh favourite is lemon juice and black pepper. This hits the taste-buds on all sides (sour, sweet and hot), so makes a big impact. Try it. Couldn't be easier!

STARTER 13

Fish soup with rouille toasts

2 red peppers, cored, de-seeded and chopped
2 large Spanish onions, peeled
2 fennel bulbs, with feathery tops
1 old potato, peeled and finely chopped
6 tbsp olive oil
4 garlic cloves, peeled and crushed
450 g (1 lb) mussels, cleaned and bearded
675 g (1½ lb) mixed white fish
1 crab
450 g (1 lb) fresh squid
2–3 litres (4 pints) rich fish stock (see page 154)
1 tsp saffron strands
sea salt and freshly ground black pepper

Rouille toasts
4 tbsp fresh mayonnaise (see page 153)
3 hard-boiled egg yolks, mashed
2 garlic cloves, peeled and crushed
a generous pinch of cayenne pepper
1 baguette, cut into rounds

To serve
grated Gruyère
a small dash of chilli sherry (optional – see page 143)

Soup method

Chop all the vegetables finely and sauté in the olive oil slowly over a low heat for 20 minutes until soft. Then add the garlic, the mussels (discarding the shells when opened and any mussels where the shells do not open during cooking), the fish, crab flesh and squid. Cook on for another 5 minutes.

Next, pour the stock over the mixture, add the saffron, and simmer for about 30 minutes. Season and then liquidize the soup until smooth with some coarse texture.

Toasts method

Mix the rouille ingredients together. Toast the bread slices and spread the rouille on the toasted baguette rounds.

To serve

Float the rouille toasts in the soup, with a sprinkling of grated Gruyère (or Parmesan) on top. Add a drop or two of chilli sherry if you dare.

MAIN COURSE 13

Roast glazed spiced gammon

Suggested accompaniments
Matchstick potatoes with anchovies and cream (see page147)
Bobby beans with a warm lemon and caper vinaigrette (see page 142)

Gammons naturally contain substantial amounts of salt from the brine used in the pickling process, so the joint must be soaked in cold water for at least 8 hours, completely covered, changing the water a few times. The joint may be bone-in or de-boned, rolled and tied. Either way, soaking is a *must*, so you don't get a poor result when you eat.

Smoked gammons are fine for taste, but will be naturally a little drier from the smoking process, so the cooking time should be reduced slightly.

> 1 gammon joint (or half gammon), up to about
>   3 kg (7 lb)
> 1 carton apple juice or 1 bottle cider
> 20 black peppercorns
> 6 cloves
> 2 cinnamon sticks
> 4 bay leaves
> 2 whole onions, peeled
>
> Glaze
> 110 g (4 oz) Dijon mustard (grainy is OK)
> 1 small jar clear honey (250g/8 oz)
> 110 g (4 oz) demerara sugar

Method

After soaking, drain the joint and place skin side down into a large saucepan with the apple juice or cider, and fill with cold water to cover the meat. Add the spices, bay leaves and onions and bring to the boil. Skim off any scum or froth and discard, then reduce heat to a slow simmer and, with a lid on the pot, simmer on very low for at least 1½ hours (for half gammons) and up to 2 hours (for whole).

When cooked, remove and drain, with the skin side uppermost. Gently remove the skin with a very sharp knife, leaving most of the fat on. Score the fat lightly in a fine criss-cross diamond pattern. This will prevent the glaze from running off.

Mix the mustard, honey and sugar together, then cover the joint with this, spreading it evenly.

In a large roasting tin, roast in the oven (180–190°C/ 350–375°F/Gas 4–5) for about 40–50 minutes depending on size. Don't set the oven too hot (and

check it is running at the correct temperature with an oven thermometer) or the sugars will burn black and taste bitter. The gammon should have a golden-brown colour. This can be achieved easily by basting the sugars on to the joint at regular intervals.

Remove from the oven and cover with foil. Leave to rest for about 20 minutes before carving.

DESSERT 13

American breakfast cake

This cake can also be served and enjoyed with a good Colombian coffee at breakfast time or mid-morning.

> 300 g (10 oz) plain flour
> 25 g (1 oz) caster sugar
> 3 tsp baking powder
> a pinch of salt
> 110 g (4 oz) slightly salted butter
> 50 g (2 oz) mild Cheddar cheese, grated
> milk to moisten
> 4 eating apples (Braeburn are good)
> 50–80 g (2–3 oz) soft brown sugar
> ½ tsp powdered cinnamon
> a little melted butter

Sieve the flour, caster sugar, baking powder and salt together into a bowl. Rub in the butter, then mix in the cheese. Add enough milk to moisten the mixture and form a soft but not sticky dough. Knead the dough lightly on a floured board. Pat it out on to an ungreased Swiss roll tin about 18 × 25 cm (7 × 10 in).

Pare, core and thinly slice the apples, and arrange on the dough. Sprinkle with the brown sugar and

cinnamon, brush with the melted butter, and bake for 25 minutes at 220°C/425°F/Gas 7. Serve warm.

STARTER 14

Singapore laksa

Unlike European chefs who delight in praise – and will show you the secrets of their cuisine – oriental chefs guard their recipes jealously and view foreigners' interest in the ingredients and method as suspicious. Mick first tasted this spicy soup in a Malaysian restaurant and on enquiring as to the contents, was told 'Soup!' This prompted him to analyse and use his taste-buds to separate out and discern all the varying ingredients.

The way to get the right balance of flavour is to taste it after the addition of each major ingredient, viz. the stock, followed by the coconut milk, ginger and garlic, checking for 'hotness' last.

2 Spanish onions, peeled and chopped into
    5 mm (¼ in) dice
3 tbsp peanut oil
2.3 litres (4 pints) strong chicken stock
    (see page 155)
50 g (2 oz) dried shrimp powder (laksa powder)
juice of 1 lime
2 × 400 g (14 oz) cans coconut milk
1 × 5 cm (2 in) piece fresh ginger, peeled
2 garlic cloves, peeled and finely chopped
4 chicken thighs, de-boned with skin
sea salt and freshly ground black pepper
4 medium squids, bodies about 20 cm (8 in)
    long, or 8 small, skinned, gutted and
    cleaned

1 small dash chilli oil
a small handful of laksa leaves, washed and
    chopped *
50 g (2 oz) vermicelli-style rice noodles
225 g (8 oz) fresh beansprouts
1 bunch spring onions, with green flags, roughly
    chopped

* Laksa leaves are known as Dao Kasom in Malay and Pael (pronounced 'pell') in Thai. Good oriental shops should stock them.

Method

In a large saucepan, on a high heat, sauté the onion quickly in the oil until the edges of the onion are turning dark brown. Then add the stock, laksa powder and lime juice and bring to the boil. Whisk in the cans of coconut milk (including the waxy layer of coconut cream that sets on the surface), and continue to whisk until the cream is incorporated into the stock. Add the ginger and garlic and stir. Remove from the heat.

Next grill or fry the seasoned chicken so that the skin is cooked well, then slice thinly into the soup. Slice the squids small (criss-crossing the skin on the inside surface will ensure the pieces curl up neatly, displaying the cross-hatched surface in true oriental fashion). Add the squid to the soup, with the chilli oil, laksa leaves and noodles and simmer for 5 minutes. Next add the beansprouts and spring onions and turn off the heat.

The noodles should be soft and completely cooked without being mushy. Serve in large bowls with chopsticks for the pieces and china soup spoons to drink the rich soup. This is a surprisingly filling dish, and can be used as a single-course supper if bigger bowls are used.

Chicken satay with cucumber, red rice and gado gado salad

8 × 175 g (6 oz) chicken fillets

2 tbsp soy sauce

4 tbsp coconut milk

1 large long ridge-type cucumber, cut into small
    cubes

900 g (2 lb) red Camargue rice *

Satay sauce

225 g (8 oz) shelled peanuts

1½ tbsp coconut oil

1 medium onion, peeled and finely chopped

1 garlic clove, peeled and finely chopped

2 tsp mild curry powder

2 small red chillies, de-seeded and finely
    chopped

1 tbsp soy sauce

1 tbsp lime juice

1 tsp palm or brown sugar

475 ml (16 fl oz) water

* As a change from plain white or basmati rice, we
have suggested you use red rice. It has a nutty texture
and is quite flavoursome on its own. The chicken
and sauce are quite spicy, so there's no need to jazz
it up in any way. Although Indonesia has its own
speciality types of rice (e.g. black rice and red), good
supermarkets have this Camargue rice easily available in packets. Red rice has a nature rather like
brown rice, so you have to cook it more slowly and let
it steam towards the end to ensure a soft centre.

Chicken method

The chicken should be cut into 2 cm (¾ in) cubes
and placed on wooden skewers that have been soaked
in warm water, then immersed in a marinade of the
mixed soy and coconut milk. After an hour or so they
can be char-grilled or placed under your domestic
grill at the highest temperature. Serve with the satay
sauce, the small cubes of cucumber, and the rice.

Satay sauce method

Process the nuts in a blender until fine. Heat the oil
in a heavy-based saucepan and fry the onion and
garlic on a medium heat for about 1 minute. Add the
curry powder and peanuts and fry for a further 3
minutes, turning the mixture carefully to prevent
catching or sticking and burning.

Add the chillies, soy, lime juice, sugar and water
and bring to a boil, then place on a very low heat and
simmer for 15 minutes, stirring frequently. When
cooked and left to get cold the sauce will thicken and
stiffen into a paste-like consistency, so serve this
sauce warm and fluid.

Gado gado salad

This is Indonesia's version of the 'warm salad',
and you can vary the vegetables used according to
the season. However, the ones usually used are
beansprouts, potatoes, green beans, carrots and
white cabbage. Here we have added sugar-snap peas
and, to give a crispy texture, apple.

Peanut sauce

120 ml (4 fl oz) peanut or sunflower oil

4 garlic cloves, peeled and chopped

350 g (12 oz) shelled peanuts, processed to a
    coarse powder

4 tbsp mild curry powder

1 tbsp sweet mango chutney

1 small chilli, de-seeded and finely chopped
120 ml (4 fl oz) lime juice
4 tbsp soy sauce
600 ml (1 pint) coconut cream
475 ml (16 fl oz) water

Vegetables
450 g (1 lb) white cabbage, cut into narrow
    strips
4 carrots, cut into thick dice
24 small new potatoes, peeled and boiled
350 g (12 oz) beansprouts
350 g (12 oz) sugar-snap peas, trimmed
175 g (6 oz) broccoli florets, cut small

Method

To make the sauce, heat the oil in a heavy-based saucepan over a medium heat, add the garlic and the nuts and cook for 2 minutes, stirring frequently. Add the curry powder, the chutney and chilli and cook on for another 2 or 3 minutes. Next, add the lime juice, soy, coconut cream and water and simmer for 30 minutes, stirring frequently to prevent sticking and burning.

The idea of the salad is to blanch all the vegetables in boiling water (the potatoes having been pre-cooked to make them tender) for about 2–3 minutes so that they do not lose their crunchiness. They are then drained thoroughly and served on a warm plate, with the peanut sauce on top.

DESSERT 14

Jackfruit fritters

Jackfruit are large Far Eastern fruits, now available in oriental supermarkets. They look like huge green rugby balls with a greeny knobbly skin, and the flesh resembles the colour and texture of pineapple, but has a much more delicate and distinctive taste. If you can't get jackfruit readily, pineapple makes a reasonable substitute.

Batter
1 tsp fresh yeast
90 ml (3 fl oz) fresh whole milk
60 ml (2 fl oz) ale (light or pale)
1 small egg yolk
a pinch of sea salt
150 g (5 oz) plain flour
2 tbsp peanut oil
2 small egg whites

Fritters
½–1 jackfruit (about 4 kg)
110 g (4 oz) caster sugar
juice of 1 lemon
60 ml (2 fl oz) kirsch
oil for deep-frying
icing or fine caster sugar for serving

Batter method

Beat together the yeast with the milk, and then add the ale, egg yolk and salt. Stir in the flour carefully, and whisk until there are no lumps and the mixture is smooth. Next whisk in the oil. Cover the batter with a damp cloth and leave to rest at room temperature for about 2½–3 hours.

Jackfruit method

Peel the jackfruit and make triangular-shaped fans of fruit about 5 mm (¼ in) thick. Steep the fruits in a bowl with the sugar, lemon juice and the kirsch for 1 hour.

Fritter method

To cook, beat the egg whites until stiff, fold into the batter and dip pieces of fruit into the batter. Deep-fry at 180–200°C/350–400°F for a few minutes – they should rise to the surface when cooked – when they will be golden-brown. Drain on absorbent kitchen paper and dust with icing sugar. Keep warm whilst waiting for the rest to be done. Delicious eaten alone or with a fruit coulis to dip into.

STARTER 15

Bruschetta with marinated grilled squid and a green salsa

Bruschetta is the beginning of a typical Roman-style meal, and consists basically of a slice of rustic bread, e.g. ciabatta, grilled on (ideally) a charcoal grill, then rubbed on one side with a half clove of garlic and then dressed with premium quality extra-virgin olive oil.

In the Abruzzo, small squids are eaten sliced thinly, raw, with dressing, but we have adapted this for the more squeamish palate by char-grilling them lightly.

Green salsa
a large handful of flat-leafed parsley, chopped
6 sprigs coriander, leaves only
6 rocket leaves
1 garlic clove, peeled
1 spring onion, including green 'flags', finely chopped
8 anchovy fillets, drained and chopped
1 tsp Dijon mustard
1 tsp lime juice

250 ml (8 fl oz) extra-virgin olive oil
salt and freshly ground black pepper

Squid
10 small squids, about 15 cm (6 in) long or so, skinned, gutted and cleaned
sea salt and freshly ground black pepper
8 tbsp premium quality extra-virgin olive oil
juice of 2 lemons
3 sweet mild onions, peeled and very thinly sliced
grated zest of 1 lemon

To serve
8 large slices rustic white bread, e.g. ciabatta, cut diagonally
2 garlic cloves, peeled and halved

Salsa method

Blitz the first six items in a processor until smooth and then add the mustard and lime juice and stir in well. Now slowly whisk in the olive oil with a balloon whisk, until all is incorporated. Season to taste.

Squid method

Cut the squids into two main parts, the body and the tentacles (removing the tentacles by cutting just below the eyes and removing the hard beak of the mouth). Season them, oil them lightly in 2 tbsp of the oil and char-grill (or conventionally grill) over a high heat for a few minutes only, turning them carefully to ensure even cooking. Do not overdo them or they will become tough and chewy. Then slice them and put them into a marinade of the lemon juice and half the oil. Add the sliced onions and lemon zest. Season lightly. Leave to marinate for 1 hour.

To serve

Rub one side of the grilled breads with a cut half of garlic and then dress with the remaining oil. Place pieces of the squid (and onion, if you like) on to the bruschetta, and spoon some of the salsa sauce around the plate for dipping.

MAIN COURSE 15

Grilled rump of lamb with button onions

Suggested accompaniment
Garlic mashed potato (see page 146)
Braised beans (see page 142)

Marinade
½ bottle red wine
4 bay leaves
a few sprigs of fresh rosemary and fresh thyme, chopped
4 garlic cloves, peeled and crushed

Lamb
8 large pieces of lamb rump, about 250 g (9 oz) uncooked weight each, trimmed
6 tbsp olive oil
sea salt and freshly ground black pepper

Button onions
675 g (1½ lb) button onions, peeled
25 g (1 oz) unsalted butter
1 tbsp olive oil

Lamb method 1

Put the marinade ingredients into a dish and place the lamb steaks into it. Rest in the marinade for 3–4 hours, turning them every so often to evenly soak the meat. Then strain off the marinade, discard the herbs (reserving some of the rosemary for the beans), and use the liquid for cooking the beans (see page 142).

Lamb method 2

Oil each piece of rump lightly with olive oil, season with salt and pepper and grill on a high heat for about 5 minutes each side or until the lamb is cooked medium rare, that is with a pink centre and pink juices, but no blood running out when skewered.

Button onion method

Preheat the oven to 200°C/400°F/Gas 6. Sauté the onions in the butter and oil until browned, then put in the oven for 20–30 minutes or until tender.

To serve

Serve on a bed of garlic mashed potato with the button onions and casseroled beans on the side.

DESSERT 15

Crème brûlée with candied ginger and Stroh rum

600 ml (1 pint) double cream
3 vanilla pods, split
8 egg yolks
2 tbsp caster sugar
2 tbsp Stroh rum
unsalted butter for greasing
3 pieces of candied stem ginger, thinly sliced
demerara sugar for caramel lid *

* Do not use soft brown muscovado-type sugar as this burns black without caramelizing properly.

Method

Place the cream and the vanilla pods in a high-sided saucepan. Heat slowly, stirring occasionally, to just below boiling point (don't let the cream boil). Set aside to cool slightly for 5 minutes.

Now preheat the oven to 160–180°C/325–350°F/Gas 3–4.

Whisk the egg yolks with the sugar until creamy in consistency, and then stir in the warm cream and the rum.

Grease eight ramekins and fill with the mixture to about 1 cm (½ in) from the top lip. Place foil squares over the pots and smooth down the sides so the foil lid is straight and level (i.e. not touching the mixture).

Place the ramekins, evenly spaced, into a hot water bain-marie and then into the oven for 15–17 minutes. Test one after 15 minutes by peeking in under the foil lid and gently tapping to check its solidity: prod the surface gently with your finger (don't break the skin of the custard), and ascertain whether it's too sloppy and needs another few minutes.

Allow to cool, then refrigerate. (The brûlées can be prepared up to this point the day before.) Uncover and place four or five thinly sliced slivers of the candied ginger on top of each custard and sprinkle a generous layer of sugar 3–5 mm (⅛–¼ in) thick evenly over the entire surface.

Preheat the grill to its maximum until red-hot, and then get the ramekins as close to the heat as possible. Watch the sugar melting and turning into caramel. You have to remove the pots immediately to stop the cream layer underneath boiling. Turn the pots around and rotate the less brown areas to catch the heat best. Allow to cool completely before serving.

Rocket salad with pan-fried duck, poached egg and truffle oil

3 large magret duck breasts
olive oil
sea salt and ground white pepper
40 g (1½ oz) mixed salad leaves (50 per cent
*   rocket, with some oakleaf, frisée and white*
*   batavia or lamb's lettuce)*
vinaigrette for dressing leaves (see page 154)
8 small eggs
1 tsp white Alba truffle oil
freshly ground black pepper

Method

The duck breast should be trimmed of excess skin, sinews and fat around the edges. Lightly oil with olive oil, season with salt and white pepper, and leave to reach room temperature.

Meanwhile, dress the leaves very lightly with the vinaigrette.

Preheat the oven to 220–230°C/425–450°F/Gas 7–8.

To cook the duck, simply heat a heavy-based frying pan with about 1 tbsp olive oil and sear the breasts all over for a few minutes each side. Let rest on a baking tray. When all the breasts have been sealed, place them in the oven for 10–13 minutes (or thereabouts), or until the juices are pink but not bloody. Please remember that duck has a lean flesh (despite a very fatty skin) and if left for only a couple of minutes too long will get hard, with an unappetizing grey colour and chewy texture. They should be cooked medium rare. Rest the breasts on a warm plate to 'set' the flesh. Quickly poach the eggs. Slice the duck very thinly and arrange in a circle around a mound of leaves with the egg on top. A few drops of truffle oil on the hot egg when cut into will release the aromatic yolk around the plate, and a final grind of black pepper will complete the dish.

MAIN COURSE 16

Pot-roast beef with field mushrooms and red wine

Suggested accompaniment
Mashed potato with soured cream and spring onions
(see page 147)

Pot-roast has always been regarded as the 'poor relation' of the kitchen repertoire – quite unfairly, in our opinion – but the result will be only as good as the quality of your meat. So ensure your butcher provides prime quality.

1.8 kg (4 lb) rolled sirloin of beef
150 g (5 oz) lean unsmoked bacon, cut into
*   lardons*
6 tbsp olive oil
4 tomatoes, skinned and de-seeded
900 g (2 lb) flat open-cup field mushrooms
1 tbsp smooth German mustard
salt and freshly ground black pepper

Marinade
3 garlic cloves, peeled and crushed
4 bay leaves
1 bottle Shiraz-type red wine
1 tsp brown sugar
3 Spanish onions, peeled and chopped
3 carrots, cut into thin rounds
1 bouquet garni (parsley stems, celery, leek flags,
*   thyme, oregano and 1 tsp grated orange zest)*

Method

Soak the beef overnight in the marinade. Next day, drain and pat dry the meat, reserving the marinade with all its ingredients. Strain the marinade, keeping the vegetables separate.

In a large casserole pot with a heavy base, sauté the marinade onion and the bacon in the olive oil on a high heat until the fat starts to run from the lardons. Add the beef, and brown on all sides. When the meat is fully browned, add the marinade vegetables and bouquet garni, plus some of the reserved marinade wine to deglaze the bottom of the pan. Turn the meat over, and add the tomatoes and mushrooms. Cover with a lid and reduce the heat to low. The liquids will start to evaporate slowly. The idea here (instead of the traditional large volume of liquid that is decanted at the end and reduced separately), is to have just enough liquid to prevent scorching of the meat, which means it needs to be continually replenished. As this evaporates, so the juices in the pan concentrate and enrich as the joint cooks on. The only snag is that it needs pretty constant attention. Allow half an hour per 450 g (1 lb) of meat for cooking time.

About halfway through the cooking period, add the mustard, and check the seasoning.

Armagnac and prune tart

This tart tastes good warm or cold.

Pastry
225 g (8 oz) cold unsalted butter
110 g (4 oz) icing sugar
a pinch of sea salt
2 small egg yolks
300 g (10 oz) plain flour
a few drops of vanilla essence

Filling
*450 g (1 lb) Californian prunes ***
90 ml (3 fl oz) Armagnac
150 g (5 oz) caster sugar
500 ml (18 fl oz) double cream
2 small eggs

* Choose the 'moist'-style of ready-to-eat prunes such as Sunsweet, which come already de-stoned. (If you cannot get these, take out the stones by making a slit along one side with a sharp knife, removing the pits while trying not to destroy the overall shape of the fruits.)

Pastry method

In a large bowl, cut the butter into small chunks with two knives using a criss-cross action, then sift in the icing sugar with the salt. Work with your fingertips until the mixture is blended together and resembles breadcrumbs.

Add the egg yolks, stir around briskly and sift the flour on top, working the ingredients together with spoon. Add the vanilla essence and using your hands roll the pastry into a round ball, taking care not to overwork it.* It should just be 'gathered' together, rolled into a ball and left to chill in the fridge for a couple of hours in a polythene bag.

* *The best results are got by working the pastry crumbs well, but once the egg yolks and flour are added, a delicate touch is required.*

Tart method

Soak the prunes in the Armagnac overnight preferably, or for at least a couple of hours, while the pastry is chilling and resting.

Roll out the rested pastry to a thickness of 3 mm (⅛ in) on a lightly floured surface. Grease a 25 cm (10 in) tart tin and line with the pastry. Crimp up the top edge of the pastry so it protrudes slightly above the top of the ring, then cut off any excess. Line the base and sides of the pastry with silicone baking parchment, fill with baking beans and blind-bake in the preheated oven (220°C/450°F/Gas 6) for 10 minutes, ensuring the top edge of the tart pastry does not over-colour. Reduce the temperature to 190°C/375°F/Gas 5, remove the beans and paper, and bake on for another 5 minutes. Cool a little.

Cut the prunes in half to make flat 'discs' and layer over the finished pastry to a depth of about 1–2 cm (½–¾ in). Beat together the sugar, cream and eggs and pour over the prune layer. (Any Armagnac and prune juices left over after the fruits have been cut can be added to the cream and egg mix.) Place in the oven, again still at the lower temperature, for 20 minutes until the custard cream has set. Serve warm or cold with a light dusting of icing sugar.

Ceviche of monkfish with chillies and orange

Ceviche is a method of 'cooking' fish without heat, using the fruit acids in citrus fruits to soften and 'cook' the fish in a marinade.

Monkfish is a firm white fish that has increased in popularity and, accordingly, price in the 90s. Historically, it was so spectacularly ugly that fishmongers tended never to let customers see its terrifying head, but displayed its skinned tail only. Monkfish is popular for two main reasons other than flavour. The flesh is firm and meat-like (without the oiliness of comparable firm-fleshed fishes such as tuna or swordfish) and it does not have a fine mesh of bones, only a central cartilaginous spine that is easily removed leaving two neat tapering cylinders of meat. Consequently, it is a suitable choice whenever a recipe calls for fish to be turned on a grill without falling apart into flakes or, as here, in a ceviche.

1.4 kg (3 lb) monkfish fillet
3 navel oranges
1 grapefruit
juice of 6 limes
2 red chillies, de-seeded and finely chopped
a handful of chopped fresh coriander leaves
4 tbsp virgin olive oil
sea salt and freshly ground black pepper
1 level tsp caster sugar
1 large escarole lettuce, lightly dressed with a
  virgin olive oil

Method

Trim the monkfish of all skin and sinews, and slice into 5 mm (¼ in) thick discs. (The flesh will shrink slightly on marination.)

Peel and trim thin segments of orange and grapefruit (peeling off the segment membranes), and mix with the fish, along with the lime juice and chilli. Allow to rest for about 1 hour minimum, until the fish has become more opaque looking, and then add the coriander, oil, salt, pepper and sugar.

To serve, use a slotted spoon, and spoon the fish on to some crisp, freshly dressed salad leaves and eat immediately. Remember, if this dish is plated up too early, the juices from the fish will wilt the salad leaves.

MAIN COURSE 17

Grilled red snapper fillets and prawns with tequila mayonnaise

Tequila mayonnaise
½ tsp freshly ground black pepper
1 tsp dry mustard powder
1½ tsp sea salt
1 tbsp tequila
3 tsp fresh lime juice
2 tsp Cointreau
grated zest and juice of 2 medium oranges
4 egg yolks
300 ml (½ pint) corn oil

Fish
5 tbsp olive oil
8 large red snapper fillets

plain flour
sea salt and freshly ground black pepper
450 g (1 lb) green shelled prawns
1 red chilli, de-seeded and finely chopped
about 120 ml (4 fl oz) white wine
juice of 2 lemons
4 tbsp freshly chopped parsley

Mayonnaise method

Combine all the ingredients except for the oil in a processor, and blend until smooth. Keeping the machine running on full power, pour in the oil in a reasonably quick, smooth stream. Check seasonings and adjust as necessary. Will keep in a plastic-covered container in the fridge for three days.

Fish method

Preheat the oven to 220°C/425°F/Gas 7.

Ensure all the snapper fillets have the fine bones removed (strong tweezers or electrical pliers are useful here).

Heat a large heavy-based frying pan on a medium to high heat and pour 3 tbsp olive oil into the pan to heat up. Meanwhile, dust the top side of each fillet lightly with plain flour, season with salt and pepper, and pan-fry presentation- or flesh-side down for about 2–3 minutes, adding the prawns and the chilli after 1 minute, until the fish has a light golden-brown colour. Turn the fillets over to cook the back or the underside, and stir the prawns around to ensure even cooking.

Deglaze the pan with the white wine and place in the oven for 2–3 minutes.

To serve

To serve, sprinkle the fish fillets with lemon juice and freshly chopped parsley, and offer tequila mayonnaise on the side.

DESSERT 17

Apple layer pudding

This pudding has to be started two days before and is thus perfect for spreading the burden of preparation on the day. You will need a 1.5–2 litre (2½–3½ pint) mould, such as a pudding basin.

Zest
2 oranges, washed
80 g (3 oz) caster sugar
200 ml (7 fl oz) water

Pudding
20 small Granny Smith or Braeburn apples,
  peeled, halved and cored
150 g (5 oz) caster sugar

Zest method

Pare the peel finely off the oranges, and slice into very fine strips. Simmer with the sugar and water over a low heat until almost crystallized. It will resemble candied peel.

Pudding method

Slice the halved apples 2–3 mm (⅛ in) thick on a mandoline. The idea is to create an interlocking spiral of apple slices in the bowl with the long edge on the outside of the mould, until the layers overlap and have built up to about 4 cm (1½ in) above the edge of the mould. As you complete each layer, scatter 1 tsp sugar and some of the zest over all the surface (keeping some of the zest back for later), building up in opposite directions, and pressing down to ensure solid packing. Now cover with two layers of foil and allow to rest overnight.*

* *Don't worry if the apple discolours a little – this won't matter when the pud is cooked.*

Next day, leaving the foil in place, bake the mould in an oven in a bain-marie for 6 hours (at 150°C/300°F/Gas 2). During this time, a great deal of water will evaporate and the fruit pile will collapse down. After cooking, allow to cool, then place the mould in the fridge, with the cover intact, for 12 hours to firm up. Then turn out of the mould on to a curved-bottom plate. The hollow that appears at the top can hold fresh cream and some grated zest. The 'cake' can be cut into thin wedges using a very sharp knife.

STARTER 18

Stracciatella Romana with egg and lemon

The basis of this soup is a very strong-flavoured chicken and beef broth. Cooks in each region of Italy vary the constituents, but basically the soup is created by whisking nutmeg and lemon zest into the stock. You can vary it yourself, adding, say, mushrooms to give a different flavour, according to the season.

1 brisket of beef, about 1.8 kg (4 lb)
1 whole boiling chicken, with giblets
4 carrots
2 onions
2 leeks
6 garlic cloves
1 bunch parsley stalks
6 black peppercorns

2 rashers streaky bacon, rinds on
2 cloves
2 bay leaves
4.5 litres (8 pints) water
sea salt and freshly ground black pepper
6 eggs
a generous pinch of freshly grated nutmeg
zest of 2 lemons
freshly grated Parmesan

Method

Place all the ingredients up to and including the water together in a big stock pan and bring to the boil, then reduce to a slow simmer. Remove and skim off any scum that rises to the surface, and keep the simmer very low. This means you'll get a clearish soup without going through any of the traditional consommé 'clearing' methods. Remember, a soup that's boiling will give a cloudy result. When finished (about 3 hours), lift off any oil that has floated to the surface, using kitchen paper. This absorbs the oil and the damp paper sheets can then be discarded. Drain, filter through a fine conical sieve, and season with salt and pepper. The stock can be stored for five days in a fridge or frozen for up to three months.

To serve, simply whisk the eggs in a bowl with the nutmeg and lemon zest, and stir into the stock. The eggs will solidify into strands and then the soup can be given a topping of grated Parmesan.

Pork Milanese with linguine, peppers and courgettes

Tradition favours the use of veal for schnitzels, but you run the risk of trading taste for texture. With pork, you can have both a soft texture and a big reading on the Nosh-O-Meter. The problem is mainly that pork fillets are small in cross section, and even if beaten quite thin and flat will only make a circle of meat about 13 cm (5 in) in diameter. By 'butterfly cutting' the fillet you can stretch the potential size of the piece to an impressive and respectable 23–25 cm (9–10 in), depending on your dexterity with a knife.

By cutting almost through each slice and then upturning the fillet and repeating the process on the other side – slightly further down – you can make a 'zig-zag' of fillet, which, when laid flat and pressed, beaten or rolled, will make a large-sized fillet.

Pork
8 portions of best pork fillet, about 175 g (6 oz)
  per person
juice of 3 lemons
3 garlic cloves, peeled and crushed
sea salt, ground white pepper and freshly ground
  black pepper

plain flour for dusting
beaten egg for dipping
dried fine white breadcrumbs for coating
olive oil for shallow-frying
lemon quarters
chopped parsley

Sauce

6 spring onions, cut into large dice
3 large red peppers, skinned, cored and finely
    diced
4 small to medium courgettes,* finely diced
3 tbsp olive oil
60 ml (2 fl oz) white wine
900 ml (1½ pints) freshly made tomato and
    basil sauce (see page 32)

Linguine

350 g (12 oz) linguine (dry weight)
freshly grated Parmesan
freshly chopped basil leaves

*If you buy the courgettes too large they will have
developed seeds inside – rather like a marrow – and
their flesh will be coarse and stringy. Try to avoid
giant courgettes, and go for the small, firm ones.*

Pork method 1

To prepare the pork Milanese, dampen the flattened meat with lemon juice, then smear with a little crushed garlic and season with salt and white pepper. Press the fillets lightly into plain flour to dust them on both sides, then shake off the excess and dip into beaten egg. Slide on to a bed of white breadcrumbs, pressing firmly to coat the meat evenly. Turn over to do the other side. Let the pieces rest on a dry plate until all are ready for frying.

Sauce and pasta method

For the sauce, simply sauté the spring onion with the pepper and courgette in the olive oil over a medium heat and then add the wine and tomato and basil sauce.

Season and simmer for 10 minutes.

Cook the linguine al dente and when well drained, fold into the tomato sauce.

Pork method 2

The pork Milanese should be shallow-fried gently in good-quality olive oil for about 5 minutes on each side. When ready, it should have a golden-brown colour. The temperature of the oil is critical – too low and the breadcrumbs will not get crisp, they'll get soggy. So set the ring for medium hot and test-fry a small piece (2.5 cm/1 in square) of pork to see how it colours up.

To serve

When cooked, drain the pork on kitchen paper and serve with wedges of lemon and sprinkled with parsley and a few turns of black pepper. The pasta should be served on the side with the Parmesan and a sprinkling of basil.

DESSERT 18

Giant strawberries dipped in Belgian chocolate

Hybrid advances and hot-house technology have enabled fruit suppliers to farm strawberries almost all year round, and it is possible to get giant fruits that have a fair degree of flavour.

We practise injecting strong flavours, like

liqueurs, into fruits with hypodermic syringes, but this isn't easily done in the home, so coating the fruits is an easy alternative. Belgian chocolate has the reputation of being one of the smoothest around, and everyone has their favourites. Mick thinks the darker the better, but a good compromise for everyone is to coat half with white chocolate, with a few drops of Sambuca added to it, and half with dark with a few drops of rum or hop oil (sounds odd, we know, but it is a curiously appropriate combination).

175 g (6 oz) strawberries per person
450 g (1 lb) white chocolate, melted, with a a dash
    of Sambuca
450 g (1 lb) dark Belgian chocolate (70% cocoa
    solids), melted
a dash of dark rum or a few drops of hop oil

Method

Wash the strawberries and allow to dry thoroughly. Keep the stalks on. Using the stalks as handles, pick up each fruit and dip first one half into the white and then the other half into the dark melted chocolate. Place on a cold baking tray which has been very lightly oiled to prevent sticking, and then place in a refrigerator for an hour or so to get hardened up.

Serve straight from the fridge to prevent them thawing and sticking together.

Spicy mushroom (yam het) salad

675 g (1½ lb) fresh mushrooms
4 tbsp dark soy sauce
3 tbsp fish sauce (such as Thai nam pla)
3 tbsp lime juice
3 garlic cloves, peeled and finely chopped or
    minced
½ tsp dried red chilli powder
1 stalk lemongrass, finely chopped or minced
3 whole spring onions, finely sliced, including flags
1 celery stalk, peeled and sliced lengthways into
    fine strips
10 mint leaves, washed and chopped
1 crisp lettuce, washed and leaves separated
a handful of fresh coriander leaves

Method

Clean the mushrooms of all chaff and peat. Cut them very thinly and soak in the soy sauce for 30 minutes until the mushrooms leak juices and dilute the soy. Then place the marinated mushrooms into a mixing bowl with the fish sauce, lime juice, garlic, chilli, lemongrass, spring onions, celery and mint, and marinate for a few minutes more.

To serve, cover each plate with lettuce leaves, heap with the mushroom salad, and decorate with coriander leaves.

Roast breast of duck on pak choy and beansprouts with soy and ginger

This main course is Orient-influenced, but not so oriental that you'll go yellow or indeed need chopsticks. The duck breasts are seasoned with some anise and chilli, and the vegetables are made aromatic with soy and ginger.

4 large magret duck breasts, about 350 g (12 oz) each
2 tbsp ground aniseed (or star anise)
sea salt and ground white pepper
4 tbsp peanut oil

Duck marinade
2 tbsp peanut oil
150 ml (¼ pint) dark sweet soy sauce (kecup manis) *
4 garlic cloves, peeled and chopped
1 fresh red chilli, de-seeded and finely chopped

Vegetable stir-fry
175 g (6 oz) fresh beansprouts
4 tbsp peanut oil
2 garlic cloves, peeled and finely chopped
50 g (2 oz) fresh ginger, peeled and chopped
2 large bunches, about 675 g (1½ lb), pak choy or Chinese greens
1 bunch trimmed spring onions, sliced diagonally
1 tsp caster sugar
sea salt and ground white pepper

* *If you can't get* kecup manis *(pronounced 'ketchup marniece') you can use ordinary dark soy sauce with 2 tsp soft brown sugar mixed in as a substitute.*

Duck method

Preheat the oven to 230°C/450°F/Gas 8.

Trim the edges of the meat to remove any excess fat, skin and sinews, and cover the meat with the combined marinade ingredients. Rest the meat in this mixture for about 2 hours maximum – no more, otherwise the marinade tends to pull the juices out of the breast and render it dry and tough. Reserve the used marinade.

Next, season the duck breasts lightly with anise powder, salt and white pepper (not too much salt as the soy will have seasoned the meat well). Pan-fry them in the peanut oil over a high heat: about 3 minutes per side should seal them and then you can place the pan in the hot oven (only if handle is metal) for about 10–12 minutes, depending on the size of the breasts. (Transfer them to a baking tray if your frying-pan handle is not ovenproof.) You should aim for a result that gives a pink medium-rare colour at the centre, with plenty of juices; do not overcook, otherwise the flesh will dry out and thus make worthless eating! (Take care to use a thick oven cloth to remove the hot pan.) Let the cooked breasts rest for a few minutes in a warm place while you prepare the stir-fry (and reserve any duck juices).

Vegetable stir-fry method

Meanwhile, heat a seasoned wok (see page 11) to maximum (you will see the black oily steel discolour to a dark 'dry' matt look). When fully heated through, add the peanut oil. When smoking hot, stir-fry the garlic and ginger quickly (do not let the garlic burn) for about 10 seconds, then add the greens, beansprouts, spring onions, caster sugar, salt and white pepper and stir briskly. The greens should be

cooked through within 5 minutes or so. Again, do not overcook as the vegetables should have a good bite to them. Towards the end of the wok cooking, add a dash of the duck marinade to moisten the greens, cooking on for another 30 seconds, and then pile the mixture onto a hot serving dish. During stir-frying the greens should have released some of their moisture and helped to create a flavoursome stock in the wok. Each duck breast will have shed some juices while resting, and these can be also added to the greens mixture.

Each breast will make two portions if carved thinly and efficiently across, and looks great served on top of the greens.

DESSERT 19

Rujak (Balinese spiced fruits) with coconut rum custard

Dessert is off-the-wall. Only after a bottle of wine would anyone consider mixing fruits with chilli . . . still, nobody ever said we were saints.

about 225 g (8 oz) untrimmed weight of each of the following: papaya, pineapple, mango, banana, firm avocado and grapefruit

Sauce
juice of 10 large limes
4 tbsp palm sugar, powdered (soft dark brown will do)
1 ripe firm banana, chopped into small chunks
1 small hot chilli, de-seeded and chopped

Coconut rum custard
7 tbsp palm sugar, powdered (soft dark brown will do)
350 ml (12 fl oz) thick coconut milk
a large pinch of fine sea salt
8 medium to large eggs
a small dash of light rum

Spiced fruits and sauce method

Chill the fruits, then peel and trim into reasonably bite-sized chunks. Pour the lime juice into a blender and blitz on full speed with the sugar until combined, then add the banana and chopped chilli and blitz on half speed for 30 seconds. Pour over the fruit and mix all together gently, with bare hands to prevent the fruit getting battered and bruised. Chill for 30 minutes.

Coconut rum custard method

Beat the sugar into the coconut milk, add the salt, and then beat in the eggs until all is combined. Add the rum and mix lightly. Pour into eight buttered ramekins to 5 mm (¼ in) from the top, and cook in the oven preheated to 180°C/350°F/Gas 4 in a bain-marie. Place a clean tea towel or kitchen paper on the bottom of a high-sided roasting tray. Cover each ramekin with a square of kitchen foil, arrange equally spaced around the tray on top of the towel and fill the tray with boiling water to come halfway up the sides of each ramekin dish. Cook in the middle of the oven for about 15–18 minutes. Test for readiness by lifting the cover on one ramekin in the centre – if it is firm when tapped with a wooden spoon on the side of the dish, it's done! Serve immediately with the spiced fruits.

Gazpacho

3 red peppers

4 long green chillies

1.4 kg (3 lb) large red ripe tomatoes, de-seeded
and chopped

1 long ridge-type cucumber, peeled, seeded and
chopped

1 medium Spanish onion, peeled and chopped

10 garlic cloves, peeled and chopped

½ tsp finely grated fresh ginger

4 tbsp balsamic vinegar

5 tbsp extra-virgin olive oil

600 ml (1 pint) thick premium tomato juice

300 ml (½ pint) V8 vegetable juice

juice of 1 lemon

about 6 tbsp fresh white breadcrumbs

1 tbsp sea salt

freshly ground black pepper

1 tbsp Jamaican hot pepper sauce

Method

Roast the peppers and chillies in a hot (220°C/425°F/
Gas 7) oven to blister and remove the skins. Peel
them, de-seeFd and core, and chop into fine dice.
(To speed things up, use the clingfilm method on
page 43.)

Rest all the vegetables and ginger in a bowl with the
balsamic vinegar and olive oil for a couple of hours.
Blend everything together in a processor, using
the tomato and V8 juices to ensure all the chunks
are evenly broken down. Add the lemon juice,

breadcrumbs and seasonings and whizz around for
another few seconds and then taste. Add the hot
sauce, gradually, so as not to overdo the heat. Try not
to process the soup so fine as to render it like a purée.
Leave the texture slightly coarse or, alternatively,
process half or two-thirds of the mix very smooth
and add the coarser part last to give some texture.

Keep the soup chilled until needed. Serve in chilled
bowls with a few coriander leaves scattered on the
top. Some people add a cube or two of ice, but don't
bother. It dilutes the soup and is only really there
for effect. If the gazpacho is well made and well
chilled, it won't be in the bowl long enough to get
warm!

Duck confit on stir-fried spinach with chanterelles

Suggested accompaniment
Mashed potato with chives (see page 147)

'Confiture' or 'confit' means 'preserve', and steeping
a meat in its fat was a very traditional way of pre-
serving meats in a moist environment, rather than
drying and salting like hams.

8 duck legs

a small handful of fresh Provençale-style herbs
(chopped rosemary, thyme, bay, etc.)

2 tbsp crushed garlic

3 tbsp grated fresh ginger

a pinch of ground aniseed (or star anise)

sea salt and ground white pepper

1.5 litres (a good 2½ pints) goose fat

freshly ground black pepper

Method

Trim any excess fat from the duck legs and with a cleaver chop off the knuckle bone at the end of each. Score the skin lightly with three notches and season each leg liberally with the herbs, garlic, ginger and spice, and lightly with salt and white pepper. (Do not *over*-salt as this will draw out juices and render the duck dry.) Leave the duck legs overnight in the fridge. Cook the duck legs in the goose fat, covered, for about 1 hour at the lowest possible simmer. If bottled, meat *and* fat, in a Kilner-type jar with a sealed lid, duck confit will keep for a couple of months in the fridge.

To reheat, simply extract the legs from the fat, wipe off the excess fat, and roast in a hot oven (220°C/425°F/Gas 7) for about 10 minutes until the skin crisps up.

Serve on top of a pile of spinach with chanterelles.

Spinach with chanterelles

450 g (1 lb) chanterelles
50 g (2 oz) unsalted butter
1 garlic clove, peeled and crushed
1.4 kg (3 lb) fresh spinach, washed and tough
    stems removed
1 tsp balsamic vinegar
sea salt and freshly ground black pepper

Method

Brush the fungi clean of all grit and woody bits with a pastry brush, and cut into quarters down the middle right to the base of the stem. Pan-fry in a large wok in the butter with the garlic until quite soft. Add the spinach, a large bunch at a time. As it wilts, throw in some more until all is cooked and mixed with the chanterelles. Add a dash of balsamic vinegar and season.

Fresh date tart with Cointreau

Pastry
175 g (6 oz) unsalted butter, cubed
1½ tbsp caster sugar
1 egg
1 egg yolk
1 tbsp whole milk
1 vanilla pod, split and scraped
225 g (8 oz) plain flour

Filling
20 fresh Californian or Mejool dates, pitted and
    soaked in 4 tbsp Cointreau
7 egg yolks
650 ml (22 fl oz) double cream
65 g (2½ oz) caster sugar
1 vanilla pod, split and scraped

Pastry method

Preheat the oven to 200°C/400°F/Gas 6. Butter a 25 cm (10 in) springform tart tin with a removable base.

Make the pastry in a food processor, combining the butter, sugar, egg, egg yolk, milk and vanilla seeds and scrapings (insides only). Pulse until blended, then add the flour and process until the mixture gathers into a ball. Wrap in clingfilm and place in the fridge to chill for 2 hours.

Roll out the dough to a thickness of 3 mm (⅛ in) on a lightly floured surface, transfer to the lightly greased tin, fit snugly and cut off the overhang. Refrigerate again for 1 hour. Line the tin with baking parchment or greaseproof paper plus baking beans, and bake blind for 15–20 minutes at 200°C/400°F/

Gas 6. Reduce the oven temperature to 190°C/375°F/ Gas 5, and remove the tart base from the oven.

Filling method

While the pastry is still warm, drain the dates from their liqueur, and place them around the pastry case evenly, in a radial pattern. Next, beat the egg yolks and cream together with the sugar and vanilla seeds and scrapings until the mixture is smooth. Add the residue of the date-liqueur juices and pour all into the tin, over the dates. Bake in the centre of the oven for up to 50–60 minutes or until the mixture is just set. Check on it from 30 minutes onwards and rotate the tart to ensure even baking. Cool on a wire rack and serve at a tepid temperature. Do not refrigerate this tart as the pastry will go soggy.

not give the rich flavours associated with a newly shelled nut. The oils in walnuts, as in other nuts, rapidly oxidize in air, and eventually become rancid.

** Orange vinaigrette is the same as a traditional vinaigrette (see page 154), but uses the squeezed juice of a navel orange as a substitute for the vinegar with the addition of 1 level tsp caster sugar (optional), if the juice is somewhat sharp.

Method

Choose fresh chicory that is not discoloured; discard the outer set of leaves and trim off the brown root end. Blanched chicons should have a pale yellow top half, becoming a creamy white colour towards the root end.

Arrange the chicory in separate leaves, either radially on the starter plates or, for a more rustic look, toss together with the cheese and nuts. The orange can be peeled then sliced thinly or segmented, and arranged roughly around the plates. Dress with the orange vinaigrette.

STARTER 21

Chicory salad with Gorgonzola, walnuts and orange vinaigrette

6 large blanched heads of chicory (chicons)
225 g (8 oz) mature Gorgonzola, at room
   temperature, cubed
225 g (8 oz) fresh shelled walnuts, halved *
1 large fresh navel orange
120 ml (4 fl oz) orange vinaigrette **

* Using packet nuts is acceptable but generally does

MAIN COURSE 21

Salmon in spinach leaf parcels with sorrel mayonnaise and wild rice with toasted almonds

8 fillets of wild salmon, about 225 g (8 oz) each
sea salt and ground white pepper
110 g (4 oz) herb butter,* at room temperature
16 large fresh spinach leaves, rinsed and
   de-stalked

8 tbsp freshly made mayonnaise (see page 153)
12 large fresh sorrel leaves
sea salt
melted butter
freshly ground black pepper

⋆ *Into 110 g (4 oz) salted butter at room temperature, fold 1 tbsp finely chopped parsley, 1 tsp finely grated fresh ginger, and 1 tbsp chopped spring onion (including the green flags). Mix well together, and chill if made beforehand.*

Fish method

Remove the skin from each portion of salmon by sliding a sharp thin knife along the bottom of each fillet, taking care not to rip or distort the fish pieces, to ensure a neat shape. Season each side with sea salt and white pepper, and spread each fillet generously on the top side with the herb butter. Then wrap each fish fillet in a double layer wrapping of spinach leaves: place the fish centrally on top of a leaf and fold the sides on to the top of the fish portion; then place a second leaf flat over the top centrally, and fold the sides under to create a smooth parcel.

When all the parcels are prepared, cook them by steaming over boiling water (a trivet or a cake rack will do in a high-sided roasting pan on top of the hob). Keep the water on a gently rolling simmer and the salmon will be ready in about 6–8 minutes. To ensure the salmon is cooked enough, simply upturn one portion and prod through the bottom layer with a small paring knife to view the centre of the fillet: medium rare is our favourite, when the middle is still a little red or rare. (This way, you'll avoid spoiling the smooth appearance of the top layer.)

Mayonnaise method

Meanwhile, after making the mayo according to the recipe on page 153, wash and de-stem each sorrel leaf and whizz up together in a processor with a pinch of sea salt until the mayo has a smooth texture and is a pale green colour. Sorrel is slightly sour and has a sharp distinctive flavour that complements the salmon.

To serve

The spinach will have shrunk tight around each fillet to form a neat parcel. Serve these on top of rice (see below), brushed with melted butter and finished with a grind of black pepper and a generous dollop of sorrel mayonnaise.

Wild rice with toasted almonds

Wild rice is quite expensive, being gathered by hand – traditionally by American Indians in the lakelands of Minnesota ('land of 10,000 lakes'). A 110g (4 oz) bag may cost a few pounds, but it is rich in flavour and deserves a place in the kitchen. However, like other 'new' ingredients that captured the public's imagination, it can be done to death (like avocados in the 1970s, kiwi fruits in the 1980s and polenta and sun-dried tomatoes in the 1990s). The rule is, don't over-use the stuff, then you'll never tire of it.

150 g (5 oz) wild rice
450 g (1 lb) basmati rice
750 ml (1¼ pints) light chicken stock (see page 155)
110 g (4 oz) flaked almonds
1 tbsp melted unsalted butter
1 level tsp sea salt

Method

Wild rice takes longer to cook than basmati, being encased in a husk, so in order that they both emerge at the correct degree of tenderness at the same time, the wild grains should first be soaked in boiling water for 15 minutes.

Then they should be drained and simmered in the stock with a lid on for at least 15–20 minutes until they are partially cooked, then the basmati rice (which only takes 10 minutes or so) is added and mixed in gently. Keep the lid on, but check on the moistness, adding a dash or two of stock or boiling water if it looks dryish. Eventually all the fluid should be absorbed by the grains with the basmati fluffy and separate, and the wild grains still with a bite to them (but not too chewy and indigestible). It is for this reason we have recommended a mixture of types. Wild rice has a great nutty flavour, but should be used sparingly.

Allow the rice to dry off by turning off the flame and leaving the lid off for 5 minutes or so. Resist the temptation to stir the grains around as this will only make them cling together more: two stirrings in total – first on adding the basmati and lastly on adding the almonds – are sufficient.

Finally, brown the almonds lightly in the butter with the salt in a heavy based pan. Fold into the rice and serve.

DESSERT 21

Banana toffee pie

One of the richest stickiest desserts around – Mick has never been able to make this without stealing a slice out!

225 g (8 oz) Chocolate Hobnob biscuits, made into crumbs
175 g (6 oz) unsalted butter, melted

3 × 225 g (8 oz) cans sweetened condensed milk *
4 large ripe bananas, peeled
1 tsp demerara or granulated brown sugar
freshly grated zest of 1 lemon
300 ml (½ pint) double cream
110 g (4 oz) dark chocolate, freshly grated

* *Nestlé and Fussells are the major names to look for when buying sweetened condensed milk.*

Method

Line a 25 cm (10 in) springform cake tin with a circle of greaseproof paper. This will assist easy removal of dessert slices.

Blend the biscuit crumbs with the melted butter to make an even pie crust, which when pressed lightly down into the bottom of the tin (to a depth of 5 mm/¼ in) will form the base.

The cans of condensed milk must be immersed in boiling water and simmered, unopened and covered entirely by the water, for 1½ hours. The heat will caramelize the sugar in the milk and turn it into a brown sticky toffee. It is important that the cans are watched closely to ensure that they are covered by water *the whole time* – otherwise they will burst and shower the kitchen with boiling toffee! You have been warned! Cool a little, then spoon the warm toffee out of the cans onto the biscuit base. Spread around to an even depth of 1 cm (½ in) with a palette knife, dipping this in hot water to ensure an even coating.

Slice the bananas thinly on top, then cover with a sprinkling of the sugar. Whisk the lemon zest into the cream, then whip until stiff and spread a layer over the whole surface of the pie. Grated chocolate completes the whole effort, which registers 7.5 on the Richter scale of desserts.

STARTER 22

Capellini with wild mushrooms and truffle oil

Capellini (angel hair) is a fine-grade pasta which is good for this recipe because it cooks quickly and takes on the flavour of the sauce. We have suggested truffle oil as this works very well with mushrooms, and adds a wonderful aroma and flavour. It's not easy to buy, but if you can, it's worth it.

675 g (1½ lb) fresh mixed wild fungi (ceps, morels, chanterelles, etc.)
4 tbsp olive oil
4 garlic cloves, peeled
175 g (6 oz) shallots, peeled and finely chopped
2 large wine glasses white wine
600 ml (1 pint) fresh single cream
sea salt and ¼ tsp ground white pepper
1 handful finely chopped parsley
4 tbsp freshly grated Parmesan
600 g (1¼ lb) dry capellini pasta (fine spaghettini)
25 g (1 oz) unsalted butter

To serve
freshly grated Parmesan
freshly ground black pepper
white Alba truffle oil

Clean the fungi with a dry pastry brush to remove any chaff and, if in doubt, wash gently under cold water and drain well. Slice thinly.

Heat the olive oil in a large saucepan on a high heat until moderately hot but not smoking, then add the garlic and shallots. Take care not to brown the shallots, and stir around briskly. Add the sliced mushrooms and cook on for about 5 minutes until the mushrooms have released their juices into the pan. Add the white wine and reduce the heat to a simmer for about 2 minutes to allow the alcohol to evaporate. Remove the garlic cloves and discard them. Add the cream to the pan and simmer for another 3 minutes on a very low heat before seasoning with salt and white pepper. Add the parsley and the cheese and keep the sauce warm while the pasta is cooking.

Capellini is very fine, and will take only about 4 minutes (or less) to cook. Salt the water well,* and check near the time by removing a strand and carefully nibbling an end to see if it is al dente. It should not be soggy.

* Nick always puts a dash of oil into his pasta water, but then what does he know about cooking? (Actually, oil is sometimes useful in pasta water – for example when pre-cooking lasagne sheets, to stop layers sticking together.) The main thing is to use the biggest pot you have, with plenty of well-salted water on a ferocious boil. All pasta cooks on in its own heat after removal from the cooking pot, so don't overcook.

Drain the pasta well, and add the knob of butter to stop the strands sticking together. Fold into the mushroom sauce. Mix the sauce in well – it should coat the pasta without being runny. The dish should be served on warm plates with a generous grating of Parmesan and black pepper and a few drops of truffle oil.

Chicken Valdostana

Suggested accompaniment
Ratatouille (see page 150)

Veal and cheese are the mainstays of the Valle d'Aosta regional cuisine because of the rich pastures bordering Switzerland and the French Alps. Nowadays chicken is used instead of veal, and we have replaced the traditional Fontina with buffalo mozzarella to help create a lighter dish.

8 skinned and boned chicken breasts
sea salt and ground white pepper
plain flour for dredging
6 eggs, lightly beaten
dried white breadcrumbs
110 g (4 oz) unsalted butter
4 tbsp olive oil
8 slices prosciutto crudo
8 large slices buffalo mozzarella, 5 mm (¼ in)
*   thick minimum*
8 tbsp tomato and basil sauce (see page 32)

  To serve
freshly ground black pepper
chopped fresh basil leaves

Method

Preheat the oven to 180–190°C/350–375°F/Gas 4–5.

Each chicken breast must be beaten flat with a wooden meat mallet between two sheets of grease-proof paper until it is not more than 5 mm (¼ in) thick. Each escalope is then seasoned with salt and white pepper, dredged with plain flour, dipped into beaten egg and coated liberally with breadcrumbs.

To cook, simply melt the butter in a large frying pan with the olive oil and fry each escalope quickly for 1 minute approximately on each side on a medium heat until light golden-brown in colour. Then allow each piece to drain on absorbent kitchen paper.

Next, place a thin slice of prosciutto on top of each escalope with a piece of cheese and a spoonful of tomato and basil sauce to top it off. Then place on a metal tray and put into the oven for 3–4 minutes, just to heat the chicken through and to slightly melt the cheese. Don't overbake, however, as this will dry out the meat and the ham will start to curl up and look unsightly.

Tiramisu 'espresso forte'

This pudding (literally meaning 'pick-me-up') was made popular by the owner of the El Toula restaurant in Treviso. Basically a layered biscuit cake with mascarpone, egg, cream and liqueur, we have included two versions, Mick's favourite – which is Savoiardi with egg Marsala – and Nick's, which is made with Amaretti biscuits and brandy.

Nick's version

  Per person
1 large egg
110 g (4 oz) mascarpone cream cheese
½ tbsp caster sugar
about 3 small coffee cups espresso coffee (made
*   very strong)*

1 large cognac *
about 6 Amaretti biscuits

* You can choose an alternative spirit to cognac, such as rum, and you could sprinkle chocolate chippings or cocoa powder on the top (the latter is good on Mick's version).

Take two bowls (Bowls 1 and 2) of similar size (Bowl 2 will eventually contain the finished Tiramisu). Separate the egg and put the white into Bowl 1, the yolk into Bowl 2. In Bowl 1, whisk the egg white until it forms peaks.

Add the mascarpone and sugar to the egg yolk in Bowl 2, and whisk all together until smooth. Now put the contents of Bowl 2 into Bowl 1, and fold all together until fully blended (this is now the Tiramisu mixture).

Mix together the espresso and cognac (4:1 coffee to spirit ratio) in a separate dish. Wash Bowl 2.

Cover the bottom of Bowl 2 with some of the Tiramisu mixture. Dip some of the Amaretti biscuits into the coffee/cognac mixture so that they soak it up, and lay them on top of the layer of Tiramisu in Bowl 2. Don't oversoak the biscuits or they will disintegrate – test one by dipping and breaking in half after a few seconds. The coffee mix should have penetrated almost to the centre. Too quick and it will give a 'dry' result. Too slow and it will be mush. You have been warned!

Repeat the above two procedures until you reach the top of Bowl 2 (having filled it with alternate layers of Tiramisu and soaked biscuits) and place in the fridge.

Mick's version

Per person
1 large egg
110 g (4 oz) mascarpone cream cheese

½ tbsp caster sugar
about 6 Savoiardi biscuits *
about 3 small coffee cups espresso coffee (made very strong)
90 ml (3 fl oz) Marsala wine **

* If you can't get Savoiardi biscuits, you can use 8 boudoir (lady finger) biscuits instead.

** Marsala is a fortified dark wine from Sicily. Ensure it is the dark sweet 'egg' Marsala. Dilute it 2:1, coffee to Marsala. Don't use the pale 'thin' Tio Pepe sherry-like Marsala – it won't give the right result.

Make in exactly the same way, substituting the Savoiardi biscuits and Marsala for the Amaretti and cognac.

Tuscan bean soup

Suggested accompaniment
Foccaccia (see page 144)

Tuscany is not renowned for its pasta or risottos. Its forte is meat. The accompaniments are traditionally great vegetables, and a liberal use of herbs with distinctive local olive oils.

Beans are commmonly served with any number of meats such as game, wild boar, and grilled pork chops. As for the soups, anything the inventive Tuscans could find went in – a real seasonal chuck-it-all-in approach. The Tuscans historically used a 'fiasco', a special flask, to cook the white cannellini beans in. The word 'fiasco' has consequently passed down into our own language, and corrupted to mean a kind of ignominious result or mess. Quite unfair really, as sometimes in the kitchen a true mélange of many different items often go to make up quite a sublime result that is greater than the sum of its parts. But enough of this semantic discourse – get simmering the *minestra di fagioli*, guys!

> 225 g (8 oz) white cannellini (haricot) beans, soaked overnight in hot water, drained *
> 50 g (2 oz) smoked pork belly or pancetta, cut into lardons
> 1 medium onion, peeled and finely chopped
> 1 medium leek, washed and finely chopped
> 1 medium carrot, finely chopped
> 3 garlic cloves, peeled and chopped
> 1.75 litres (3 pints) strong chicken stock (see page 155)
> 3 tbsp Tuscan olive oil
> sea salt and freshly ground black pepper
> 4 tbsp chopped flat-leaf parsley

If you don't soak your beans thoroughly, you may have to simmer them for possibly another hour to get them soft. Don't skimp on the soaking part of the preparation!

Method

Cover the soaked beans, pork, all the vegetables and the garlic with the stock and oil and bring slowly to the boil. Simmer very gently for about 2 hours or until the beans are quite soft, but not disintegrating. Keep the mixture covered with stock at all times.

Then purée half of the bean–vegetable mix in a processor with a little of the stock until smooth, then return to the pan with the whole beans and heat gently until hot. Adjust seasoning, stir in the parsley and serve with some crusty bread (foccaccia is good) to dip in.

Roast leg of lamb with anchovies

Suggested accompaniment
Mashed potato (see page 147)

One of our favourite chefs, Simon Hopkinson, has actually given us permission to reproduce our favourite recipe from his recent book, *Roast Chicken and Other Stories* (Ebury Press)! Simon, like us, has the same enthusiasm for the essential elements at the heart of a successful dish – good-quality ingredients and a well-crafted, simple cooking process. Odd though the combination of lamb and anchovy sounds, it seems as if they were made for each other.

> 1.8 kg (4 lb) leg of lamb
> 4 large garlic cloves, peeled and sliced lengthways into 3
> a small bunch of rosemary
> 2 × 50 g (2 oz) cans anchovies, drained
> 80 g (3 oz) butter, softened
> freshly ground black pepper
> ½ bottle dry white wine
> juice of 1 lemon
> a bunch of watercress

Method

Preheat the oven to 220°C/425°F/Gas 7.

With a small sharp knife, make about twelve incisions, 5 cm (2 in) deep in the fleshy side of the joint. Insert a piece of garlic, a small sprig of rosemary and half an anchovy into each incision. Push all of them right in with your little finger.

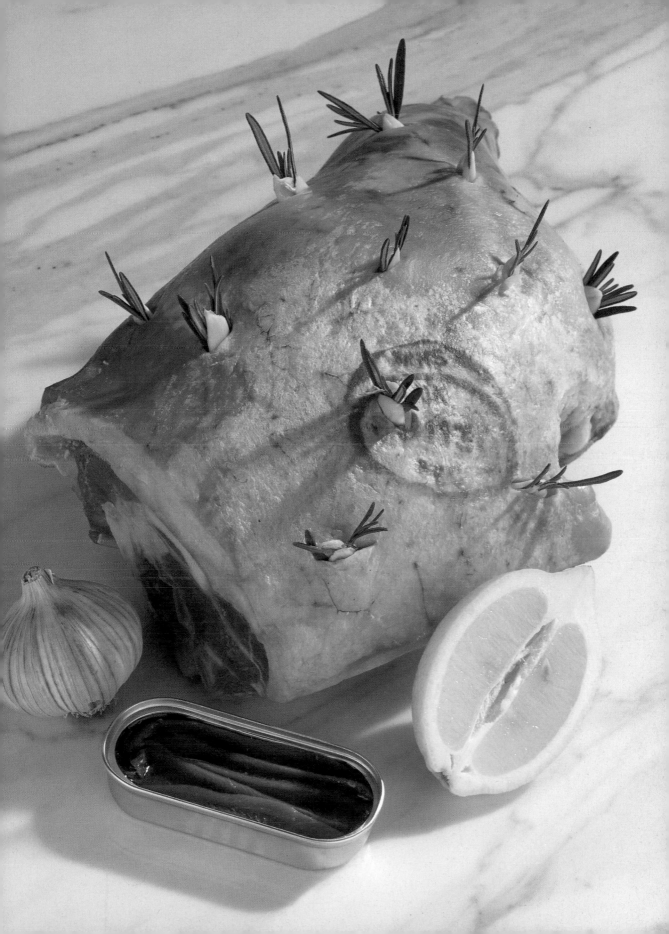

Cream the butter with the remaining anchovies and smear it all over the surface of the meat, and grind on plenty of black pepper, then place the lamb in a roasting tin and pour the wine around. Tuck in any leftover sprigs of rosemary and pour over the lemon juice.

Place in the preheated over for 15 minutes. Turn down the oven temperature to 180°C/350°F/Gas 4 and roast the lamb for a further hour or so, depending on how well done you like your meat. Baste from time to time with the wine juices.

Take out the meat and leave to rest in a warm place for 15 minutes before carving. Meanwhile, taste the juices and see if any salt is necessary – it shouldn't be because of the anchovies. During the roasting process, the wine should have reduced somewhat, and mingled with the meat juices and anchovy butter to make a delicious gravy. If you find it too thin, then a quick bubble on the hob should improve the consistency. When it comes to good food smells, this is one of the best because, as you slice it, the waft of garlic, rosemary and anchovy hits you head on. Garnish with the watercress.

Raspberry ice cream

8 egg yolks
150 g (5 oz) caster sugar
1 vanilla pod, split
750 ml (26 fl oz) whole milk
225 g (8 oz) raspberries
a dash of crème de cassis
175 ml (6 fl oz) double cream

Method

Whisk the egg yolks in a large bowl with half the sugar until the mixture goes creamy and forms ribbons when whisked around.

Squeeze out the black paste – the seeds – from the split vanilla pod, place it with the remaining sugar and the milk in a saucepan and bring to the boil. When risen, pour the hot milk onto the sugar and yolk mix, whisking vigorously. Pour the mixture back into the saucepan and place it over a very low heat, stirring continuously with a whisk until the custard thickens enough to coat the back of a spoon. Do not let the mixture sit or overheat as it will boil and produce congealed 'scrambled egg' – so keep an eye on it as you whisk. When thickened, pass the custard through a fine conical strainer and let it cool completely. Place a layer of clingfilm on top of the custard to stop a skin forming.

Wash the fruit gently, let them dry and then blitz them in a processor with the cassis. Add the cream to the fruit and process for a few seconds. Then add to the custard and mix together thoroughly. Pour into a plastic container and place in the freezer. Keep covered, and stir every hour until the ice cream is fully frozen.

To serve, allow to warm up at room temperature for 5 minutes to allow easy scooping of portions.

STARTER 24

Spiced peppers on butter-rich cornbread

3 large yellow peppers

3 large red peppers

6 spring onions, thinly sliced

1 tbsp caster sugar

1½ tsp sea salt

½ tsp freshly ground black pepper

3 tbsp ground cumin

½ tsp hot pepper sauce (to taste)

extra-virgin olive oil (to coat peppers)

Cornbread

Makes eight 10 × 5 cm (4 × 2 in) rectangles.

80 g (3 oz) finely ground yellow cornmeal

90 g (3½oz) plain strong white flour

½ tsp sea salt

1 tbsp baking powder

2 medium eggs

300 ml (½ pint) soured cream

110 g (4 oz) whole kernel blanched
sweetcorn (frozen, thawed and
drained is OK)

60 ml (2 fl oz) corn or peanut oil

60 ml (2 fl oz) slightly salted butter, melted

Spiced peppers method

Roast the peppers under a grill or preferably on top of a char-grill to char the skin. When evenly done, place under clingfilm to 'sweat' off the skin (see page 43). When cool enough to handle, de-seed the peppers, remove the cores, and slice the flesh lengthways into convenient strips.

Mix the pepper strips with the spring onions, sugar, salt, pepper, cumin and pepper sauce. When combined, add the olive oil lightly to coat the vegetables.

Serve on warm cornbread squares (see below).

Cornbread method

Preheat the oven to 200°C/400°F/Gas 6. Oil a 20 cm (8 in) square baking tin with vertical unsloping sides.

Sift and combine the cornmeal, flour, salt and baking powder into a bowl. Separately, beat the eggs until blended, then stir in the soured cream, drained sweetcorn and the oil. Pour the liquid mixture over the dry ingredients and mix until moistened. Spread into the prepared tin and bake for about 30 minutes, or until the bread shrinks away from the tin sides. It should look golden and not brown.

Before serving brush the melted butter over the cornbread and let it stand in the tin for 5 minutes to absorb the butter. Cut into rectangles and serve while still warm.

MAIN COURSE 24

Southern chicken with plantation pot salad and Nosh potato salad

This is chicken breasts, marinated in bourbon, then grilled.

8 boned and skinned chicken breasts (free-range
or corn-fed)

Marinade
400 ml (14 fl oz) bourbon whiskey
200 ml (7 fl oz) soy sauce
4 tbsp Dijon mustard
8 spring onions, with green tops, sliced
8 tsp light muscovado sugar
1 tbsp Worcestershire sauce

Method

Make four neat, shallow slits in the top side of each breast to allow the marinade to penetrate.

Mix together all of the marinade ingredients, stirring until the sugar and mustard are dissolved. Coat the chicken with the marinade, and leave to absorb it for about 1 hour at room temperature.*

* Do not marinate the meat for a longer time than 1 hour as the saltiness of the soy will draw out the natural juices and dry the chicken.

Char-grill the chicken breasts for about 8–10 minutes, depending on size and start temperature. You can place the meat under a normal grill, but ensure it has been preheated to its maximum.

Plantation pot salad

about 350 g (12 oz) varied squashes (baby courgettes, patty pan mini-squashes, yellow pumpkin, whatever is seasonal)
1 plantain, peeled
12 okra
12 baby corn
2 plum tomatoes, peeled, skinned and finely chopped
4 garlic cloves, peeled and roasted (see page 131)
sea salt and freshly ground black pepper
6 tbsp virgin olive oil

2 tbsp finely chopped flat-leaf parsley
cos lettuce divided into leaves as boats

Method

Vegetables should be sliced thinly on the longest side – the squashes and plantain, for instance. Okra can stay whole (but trim the hard stalk end). Baby corn should be halved lengthways, but after grilling. Blanch some of the vegetables just to soften them slightly. Blanch the okra for 2 minutes, the corn for 3. Then char-grill all the vegetables (apart from the tomatoes) to colour and flavour them (an ordinary grill set on maximum is OK). Combine them in a bowl with all the other ingredients, seasoning well. The mixed salad should have the consistency of a dry ratatouille, being a melangé of all the grilled ingredients, seasoning, parsley, oil and garlic. Serve in the cos leaves.

Nosh potato salad

1.4 kg (3 lb) small 'new' potatoes (Maris Piper is OK)
about 600 ml (1 pint) mayonnaise (see page 153)
4 large dill-pickled sweet and sour gherkins (German brands preferred), chopped, with pickling vinegar
4 good-quality crisp eating apples (Braeburn are good)
6 spring onions, sliced thinly on the diagonal
2 pickled jalapeño hot peppers (El Paso brand is OK), de-seeded and chopped
sea salt and freshly ground black pepper

Method

Boil the potatoes in their skins in salted water until they are soft but retain a waxy middle. Refresh immediately in iced water. When cool to the touch, peel off the skins and slice into thin 3–5 mm (⅛–¼ in) rounds.

Dilute the mayo with about 120–150 ml (4–5 fl oz) gherkin vinegar (it doesn't matter if some pickling spice goes in) and mix well. Peel, core and slice the apples into small dice. Add to the mayo with the spring onions, chopped gherkins and jalapeño, and season with salt and black pepper to taste. Add the sliced potatoes, and combine gently but thoroughly to prevent the potatoes breaking up. If the mixture looks or feels too dry, add some more dill vinegar or mayo until moist.

DESSERT 24

Pecan and apricot cookies

Pecan and apricot cookies are an unusual choice for a dessert – but after such a heavy, full-on starter and main course, a semi-sweet cookie is great with your coffee.

110 g (4 oz) slightly salted butter, at room
    temperature
110 g (4 oz) caster sugar
110 g (4 oz) light muscovado brown sugar
1 egg, beaten
120 ml (4 fl oz) corn oil
1 tsp vanilla extract
425 g (15 oz) plain flour
1 tsp baking powder
¼ tsp salt
110 g (4 oz) medium grade rolled oats (not
    instant)
110 g (4 oz) shelled pecan nuts, chopped

110 g (4 oz) shredded fresh coconut (available in
    packets)
50 g (2 oz) raisins, rinsed in warm water and
    drained
50 g (2 oz) dried apricots, chopped

Method

Preheat the oven to 180°C/350°F/Gas 4. Prepare baking trays, covering them with silicone baking parchment, ungreased.

Cream the butter, gradually adding the sugars until well blended. Beat in the egg thoroughly, followed by the oil and vanilla. (The batter may look a bit curdled at this point – don't worry!)

Sift the flour, baking powder and salt into a bowl. Stir into the butter/sugar mixture in about five or six batches. Then stir in the oats, nuts, coconut, raisins and apricots.

Shape the dough into 2.5 cm (1 in) balls and put on the baking trays 5 cm (2 in) apart.* Flatten slightly with fork tines (dipped in flour to prevent sticking), and bake for 14–15 minutes until they are dry on the top and will hold a slight impression when touched on top. Cool on racks and store in airtight containers to prevent the cookies getting soggy.

* Remember that the soft dough will spread out when heated, so leave plenty of room between the balls.

This is a menu devised by Bruce Warwick, head chef of The Groucho Club in Soho. In many ways, he is like the third 'invisible' Nosh Brother – he has worked alongside us and fed us so royally, it seemed inelegant to leave him out of the book!

STARTER 25

Confit of duck livers on cabbage ragout

Duck liver confit

900 g (2 lb) fresh duck livers (chicken livers
    may be used instead)
sea salt and freshly ground black pepper
900 ml (1½ pints) olive oil
1 garlic bulb
1 large sprig fresh thyme
1 large sprig fresh rosemary
20 black peppercorns

Cabbage ragout

175 g (6 oz) duck or goose fat
1 large white onion, peeled and cut into 5 mm
    (¼ in) dice
6 garlic cloves, peeled and crushed
300 g (10 oz) skinned smoked belly of pork,
    cut into 5 mm (¼ in) dice
1 large Savoy cabbage, stem removed,
    shredded
25 g (1 oz) fresh thyme leaves, chopped

1 bay leaf
sea salt and freshly ground black pepper

Confit method

This can be done the day before. Clean and trim the livers. Sprinkle with a little salt and pepper and leave for 4 hours in the fridge.

Put the olive oil, garlic, herbs and peppercorns into a pan and place on a high heat for 4 minutes. Remove from the heat, and leave to infuse for 30 minutes.

Reheat the oil for 8–10 minutes on a medium heat. Drop the livers in gently and leave on the heat for about 2 minutes. Remove the livers from the pan, using a slotted spoon, and allow to cool.

Cabbage method

This can also be done the day before. In a pan melt the fat, then add the onion, garlic and belly of pork and sweat for 5–6 minutes. Add the cabbage, thyme and bay leaf and season with black pepper and a pinch of salt. (Be careful with the salt as the pork will be salty.) Cook on a low flame for 1½ hours with a lid on the pan, stirring every 15 minutes or so.

To serve

Preheat the oven to 220–230°C/425–450°F/Gas 7–8. Place the livers in the oven for 3–4 minutes. Heat the cabbage in a pan for about 4–5 minutes on medium heat until hot. Place the cabbage in the centre of each plate and top with two pieces of duck liver.

Brochettes of monkfish, pancetta and rosemary with avocado couscous

Brochettes
1.6 kg (3 lb) filleted monkfish, cut into 24 large
* dice*
350 g (12 oz) pancetta, sliced
8 × 20 cm (8 in) sprigs fresh rosemary
olive oil
sea salt and freshly ground black pepper
2 lemons, cut into wedges

Couscous
300 g (10 oz) dry couscous
10 drops Tabasco
juice of 2 lemons
sea salt and black pepper
60 ml (2 fl oz) extra-virgin olive oil
100 ml (3½ fl oz) boiling water
2 avocados, cut into 5 mm (¼ in) dice
a small handful of chopped chives

Brochettes method

Wrap each piece of monkfish in a thin layer of pancetta.

Remove all the leaves from the rosemary stalks, apart from about 2.5 cm (1 in) at the tip of the stalk. Make a hole through each piece of fish with a skewer, then push a rosemary stalk through it. Allow 3 pieces of fish per stalk. Chill until ready to cook.

Couscous method

Put the dry couscous, Tabasco, extra-virgin olive oil, lemon juice and some salt and pepper into a bowl.

Mix well. Gently add the boiling water to the mix, cover with clingfilm and allow to stand in a warm place for 10 minutes. Remove the clingfilm, and add the avocado and chives.*

* Cut both at the very last minute, or the avocado will discolour and the chives will lose some of their freshness.

Lightly paint the brochettes with olive oil and season with black pepper. Cook on a preheated griddle plate on high, for 2–3 minutes each side. If you don't have a griddle plate then you can grill them but make sure you cover the rosemary leaves to prevent them burning.

To serve

To serve, place a large round pastry cutter (ideally 13 cm/5 in across and 2 cm/¾ in high) on each plate in turn. Use this as a mould. Spoon the avocado couscous into the middle of the cutter, and push down lightly with the back of a spoon. Carefully remove the cutter and place the brochettes on top. Add a wedge of lemon and serve immediately.

Hot chocolate pie

Crystallized peel
2–4 organic or unwaxed oranges
80 g (3 oz) caster sugar (twice)
200 ml (7 fl oz) water (twice)

Sauce
80 g (3 oz) milk chocolate, 70% minimum cocoa
* solids, broken into pieces*
120 ml (4 fl oz) double cream
25 g (1 oz) unsalted butter
2 tbsp water

Pie

225 g (8 oz) dark chocolate, 70% minimum
cocoa solids, broken into pieces

110 g (4 oz) unsalted butter

175 g (6 oz) caster sugar

4 eggs, separated, at room temperature

80 g (3 oz) rice flour

80 g (3 oz) ground almonds

To serve

cream

2 oranges

Crystallized peel method

Start three to four days in advance. With a potato peeler, pare just the top layer of orange peel, taking no white pith. Boil this in a syrup made from the sugar and water for 5 minutes, then dry off on a wire rack for about 4 hours. Boil up again in a fresh syrup, then dry on a wire rack until brittle (this takes about 48 hours). Pulverize in a clean coffee grinder, and store in a sealed container.

Sauce method

In a saucepan, melt all the ingredients together over a slow heat. Pour into a shallow dish 20 cm (8 in) in diameter, so that the sauce is 1 cm (½ in) thick. Allow to cool, then freeze until solid, about 6 hours.

Pie mix method

Melt the chocolate in a bowl over simmering water. Cool a little. Cream the butter and sugar together well. Add the egg yolks, then fold in the rice flour, almonds and melted chocolate. Whip the egg whites until stiff and fold in.*

* This mixture can be made in advance and refrigerated for up to a week. However, it must stand at room temperature for 1 hour prior to filling the dishes.

Grease a baking tray and eight small round dishes or ramekins. Line these but do not grease again. Fill them halfway with the pie mix, using a spoon or piping bag. Cut rounds smaller in diameter than the dishes from the frozen sauce and place in the centre. Cover with pie mix, to just below the edge of the dishes. Freeze for at least 3 hours.

Bake the dishes from frozen in a preheated oven (190°C/375°F/Gas 5) for 30–35 minutes.

To serve

Turn out from the dishes onto plates and serve with cream, fresh orange segments and dusted with the powdered orange peel.

STARTER 26

Asparagus with shaved Parmesan and extra-virgin olive oil

Asparagus can be bought all the year round now from places as far away as Peru, and everyone knows how cheap and readily available Spanish asparagus is. However, all this has detracted from the fact that the best flavoured asparagus tends to come from the new season's French and English crop in May to June, with some tolerably good American varieties arriving later in the season.

Asparagus was a vegetable that suffered greatly from the infamous overcooking styles of the old-school English hotel caterers – boiled until mushy. Thankfully, we are now more fine-tuned about technique. It is traditionally served with melted butter, a vinaigrette or warm hollandaise – all very commendable – but we have chosen the fashionable Mediterranean style.

> 3 bunches best-quality asparagus (say 3
>   portions per bunch minimum, depending
>   on size)
> 5 tbsp best-quality extra-virgin olive oil
> sea salt and freshly ground black pepper
> 110 g (4 oz) wedge best Parmesan, at room
>   temperature

Method

Cut the stalks off at the bottom where the colour changes from pale cream to green. This will remove the woody part of the stems. If the stalks are very thick (some varieties can grow as thick as your thumb), peel the bottom third with a vegetable peeler, revealing the softer, inner flesh. Also remove the dark-coloured pointed stalk flaps (they resemble flat thorns) along the shoots.*

* *Not many people know that asparagus, if prepared as above and blanched for 1 minute, is delicious cooked on a barbecue grill. It has the distinctive marks and flavour of the charcoal and seems to be crunchier. (Brush lightly with olive oil first.)*

As the tops of the shoots are very fragile compared to the tougher bottoms, it is recommended to use a proper asparagus boiling canister (vertical and cylindrical, with a wire inner basket) with 4–5 cm (1½ in) of salted boiling water in the bottom.* This will allow the lower stem to cook at a quicker rate than the tender tips. You can lay the stalks flat in a pan, but test often with a knife point to ensure that the tips are not overcooking and getting mushy. The asparagus should have some bite without being actually crunchy, and cooked enough so that the whole stem is edible and not chewy at the bottom. About 3–5

minutes is usually enough, depending on size and how tightly they are packed in the pan.

* *You can use one of those enamelled heatproof coffee pots, stems in the boiling water, tips steaming at the top.*

When tender, lift the basket out and drain the asparagus. While still warm, place the bundles on a serving dish and pour over the olive oil. Sprinkle generously with fine sea salt and some black pepper. Using a peeler, shave long, thin strips of Parmesan over the whole pile. Delicious eaten warm or cold.

MAIN COURSE 26

Calves' liver Veneziana on saffron risotto

Veneziana style means with onions, flavoured with a little sage.

> 120 ml (4 fl oz) olive oil
> 120 g (4½ oz) unsalted butter
> 1 kg (2¼ lb) onions, peeled and finely sliced
> 1 kg (2¼ lb) calves' liver, very thinly sliced
> 1 tbsp chopped fresh sage
> sea salt and freshly ground black pepper
> 2 tbsp freshly chopped parsley
>
> Saffron risotto
> 1.2 litres (2 pints) chicken stock (see page 155)
>   with a generous 2 tsp saffron strands infused
>   in it for about 15 miutes
> 2 Spanish onions, peeled and diced
> 800 g (1¾ lb) arborio (risotto) rice
> 6 tbsp good-quality olive oil
> 2 garlic cloves, peeled and chopped

1 large wine glass white wine
80 g (3 oz) Parmesan, finely grated
90 ml (3 fl oz) single cream
sea salt and freshly ground black pepper

Liver method 1

In a large frying pan, heat the oil and butter on a medium flame, and cook the onions for 2 minutes, stirring. Reduce the heat to low and cook for another 25 minutes, stirring occasionally, until the onions are very soft, sweet and just coloured.

Risotto method

Firstly, warm the chicken stock with the saffron strands until the latter release their distinctive golden-yellow colour. Reserve.

In a large pan with a heavy base, sauté the onions with the rice in the olive oil on a medium heat for about 3 minutes, stirring and turning the rice over so that it is completely sealed and goes transparent. Add the garlic and white wine and half of the infused stock. Bring to the boil and turn down the heat immediately to very low. As the rice absorbs the wine and stock, add more hot stock, a little at a time, in order not to cool the bulk down too much, and stir constantly. Risotto should be moist and yet not runny, al dente to the bite, yet not raw.

After 12 minutes or so add the cheese and cream with more hot stock being added as necessary to keep the mixture moist, and to avoid any sticking to the pan base. Then season, continuing to stir, until cooked to perfection.

Liver method 2

When the onions are cooked, drain and transfer to another pot. Raise the heat under the first pan to medium and add the liver. Fry for 2 minutes on each side with the sage. Do not overcook – the liver should have a pinkish centre. Return the onions to the pan, season, add parsley and serve on top of the risotto.

DESSERT 26

Raspberry and pecan zuppa inglese

An Italian variation on the English trifle theme, this is a very easy and rewarding dessert (guests will invariably ask for seconds). You can vary the type of nuts: toasted hazelnuts go well with strawberries, or substitute walnuts, but the sweeter pecan complements the sharpness of the raspberries. You will need a large glass trifle bowl to assemble this pudding.

Nut brittle topping
175 g (6 oz) flaked almonds
50 g (2 oz) caster sugar
25 g (1 oz) unsalted butter

Trifle
*8 small trifle sponges to line the bowl ***
*150 ml (¼ pint) egg Marsala ****
175 g (6 oz) freshly shelled pecan nuts, halved
450 g (1 lb) fresh ripe raspberries (about 4 small punnets)
1.75 litres (3 pints) fresh vanilla custard (see page 94)
600 ml (1 pint) double cream

* *We have experimented with different types of sponge and cakes, some fresh and some slightly dry. Most work quite well, even chocolate ones. The important thing is to ensure that the layer of cake is well soaked in alcohol and moist.*

** *Marsala is a fortified dark wine from Sicily.*

Ensure it is the dark sweet 'egg' Marsala. Don't use the pale 'thin' Tio Pepe sherry-like Marsala – it won't give the right result.

Method

First, make the nut brittle for the topping to give it time to cool down. Heat a clean, dry frying pan on a medium flame and swirl the flaked almonds around for a few minutes until they start to colour up a golden-brown, tossing frequently to avoid burning. Add the sugar, allow to heat up, stirring, then add the butter. Cook the sugar/butter mix, stirring frequently until it changes to a sticky toffee and has a caramel aroma. Take care not to burn the nuts meanwhile. This mixture will become a sugary lump which can be spooned out on to a sheet of grease-proof paper to cool. When cold it will resemble peanut brittle and can be crumbled up into small lumps for the topping.

While the nut brittle is cooling, place the cake sponges around the sides and base of the bowl and pour over the Marsala evenly to dampen. Sprinkle some of the pecans around the bowl (about half the nuts), and tip in all the raspberries (discarding any berries that show any sign of fur). Pour over the cold custard, smooth the top flat with a rubber spatula and spread over the remainder of the pecans evenly.

Next, whip up the double cream until stiff peaks form and spread a layer over at least 1 cm (½ in) thick. Lastly, sprinkle over the nut brittle and chill the pudding in the fridge for 1 hour before serving. This will allow the fruits to settle and the sponge to soak up all the juices completely.

Menus for the Rich

Introduction

Sometimes you'll want to entertain lavishly and produce something special for your guests. On the other hand you may be feeling self-indulgent and simply want to push the boat out. Either way, this section has something for you. We make no apology for the type of foods represented here. We have only listed those we truly like, regardless of cost.

Caviar *is* expensive, but don't let anyone tell you it's overrated. Eaten fresh, it's magnificent. (And if you want a less expensive option, try using keta, or salmon eggs.) Similarly, don't let people put you off foie gras. Recently, a vegetarian woman told Mick he was 'a horrible man', and asked 'How could you?!' etc. etc. To her and all her ilk we say 'Bollocks'. The day the Taste Police tell us what we can and can't eat is the day we pack up and go home.

In this section there is a recipe for roast rib of beef, just like the joint on the front cover. Beef has been, historically, one of the great exports from our islands, and despite a hiccup recently in our farming community, still rates as first-class stuff. Indeed, Britain has contributed top-quality genes to many of the world's beefy areas. Where would Argentinian stocks have been without it? Don't be intimidated by propaganda or politically correct pseudo-socialist thinking. Trust your taste-buds and enjoy.

Menu 27

Pan-fried king scallops with coriander and lime pesto and salad

Roast partridge breasts on a bed of Savoy cabbage

Amaretti rum truffle cake with a raspberry coulis

Menu 28

Queen scallops on a broad bean purée with a red pepper and chilli coulis

Roast beef with celeriac and potato mash and Yorkshire pudding

Baked apple with brown sugar and spices

Menu 29

Black squid ink linguine with prawns, chilli and garlic

Grilled lobster with lime and oregano butter and a green seafood sauce

Nosh rich rum cake

Menu 30

Wild mushroom soup

Breast of pheasant with orange and port

Pears poached in Beaumes de Venise

Menu 31

Soto ayam Madura

Roast suckling pig with coconut rice

Guava cheesecake

Menu 32

Pan-fried foie gras with balsamic vinegar on toasted brioche

Fillet steak marinated in black bean and teriyaki sauce

Pont-l'Évêque, Camembert and mustard fruits

Menu 33

Goose liver terrine 'foie gras' style

Beef fillet parcels with mushrooms and cognac

Figs in spiced vanilla syrup

Menu 34

Langoustine ravioli with a dry Martini and cream sauce

Rare-roast medallions of ostrich fillet on sweet potato with roast garlic and wilted spinach

Mini-Pavlova meringues with clotted cream and passionfruit

Menu 35

Bresaola, rocket and truffle cheese

Roast goose with Nosh gourmet stuffing and potato and onion rösti with bilberries

Rambutan and orange fruit salad

Menu 36

Sashimi of fresh ocean fish with a wasabi vinaigrette

Char-grilled rib-eye steak with Chinese noodles, spring onions and shiitake mushrooms

Raspberry, mascarpone and almond tart

Menu 37

Blinis with smoked eel, soured cream and Beluga caviar

Fillet of sea bass on samphire

Nosh caramelized apple pie with calvados cream

Pan-fried king scallops with coriander and lime pesto and salad

Pesto
150 ml (¼ pint) extra-virgin olive oil
110 g (4 oz) pumpkin seeds, lightly toasted in a dry pan
2 garlic cloves, peeled
juice of 1 lime
3 large handfuls coriander leaves (no stems)
sea salt and freshly ground black pepper
50 g (2 oz) Parmesan, finely grated

Salad
110 g (4 oz) mixed salad leaves (baby spinach, rocket, oakleaf, baby cos or similar, but not radicchio or iceberg)
honey dressing (see page 37)

Scallops
32 fresh diver-caught scallops, with corals attached, cleaned
sea salt and ground white pepper
olive oil

Pesto method

Blend the oil, pumpkin seeds, garlic, lime juice and coriander leaves for about 1 minute in a food processor until the mixture is fine. Season with salt and black pepper, then add the Parmesan and whizz up for another 10 seconds. Allow at least half an hour for the flavours to 'develop'. (Will keep in a fridge for two to three days if covered with olive oil.)

Salad method

Clean, drain, pick over and trim the mixed salad leaves. Toss in a big bowl with the honey dressing, then arrange on plates. Spoon a dessertspoonful of pesto on to the side (the scallops will be placed on the pesto).

Scallop method

If very large, the scallops should be cut into two discs across the 'equator' to allow for quick cooking. Season with salt and white pepper. Scallops benefit from 'resting' seasoned for some 5 minutes to remove excess water, but don't leave them any longer as they will dry out.

Heat a good solid-bottomed pan (cast-iron or black seasoned mild steel is best), add a tablespoon of olive oil and allow to get hot. Pan-fry the scallops for about 1–2 minutes on each side, depending on thickness, until slightly coloured up in brown speckles. Slide the cooked shellfish, using a palette knife or fish slice, on to the pesto on the plate.

MAIN COURSE 27

Roast partridge breasts on a bed of Savoy cabbage

Suggested accompaniments
Lyonnaise-style sauté potatoes (see page 147)
Purée of carrots with cumin butter (see page 150)

Although partridge is quite fiddly to eat when carved on the plate, and there isn't much meat apart from

the breast, it is one of the best-flavoured birds. (Second only to woodcock in Mick's opinion.) So we have chosen an easy, breast-off arrangement, with the rest of the carcass used to make a rich game stock. The livers are made into a pâté which is then served on a crouton.

It is worth noting that there is a contingency for one extra portion (i.e. nine birds for eight people). As with other small game birds (grouse etc.), you might find a bird shot in the breast will have a rather bloody aspect on being carved. So, in order to spare some embarrassment, an extra bird is required for safety.

9 fresh large partridges, plucked, drawn, heart and liver intact*
300 ml (½ pint) chicken stock (see page 155)
300 ml (½ pint) veal stock (see page 155)
150 ml (¼ pint) port
1 sprig fresh thyme
9 large long shallots, peeled
olive oil
3 garlic cloves, peeled
80 g (3 oz) unsalted butter
good cognac
sea salt and freshly ground black pepper
1 Savoy cabbage, cored, trimmed of stems, and shredded
8 × 5 cm (2 in) squares of white bread, cut into triangles diagonally

Method

Preheat the oven to 220°C/425°F/Gas 7.

Ensure each bird is free of feathers, and then singe any short stubs with a flame. Remove the livers from each cavity and set aside. Fillet out each breast piece with the skin and reserve. Chop down each carcass and roast for 15 minutes in a tray. Place in a deep saucepan, cover with the chicken and veal stocks and the port, add the thyme, and bring to the boil.

Reduce the heat to a simmer, and cook for 1 hour, gently skimming off any froth or scum. Strain through a very fine conical sieve into another saucepan and reserve. The bones can be discarded.

In a metal-handled frying pan, brown off the shallots in a little olive oil with 1 garlic clove, then place the pan in the oven for 10 minutes to roast. Remove from the oven and set aside. Now place 25 g (1 oz) butter in the frying pan, and pan-fry the partridge livers on both sides, adding a small dash of cognac at the end (you can flambé the offal if you like). Place the livers (cooked medium rare) into a food processor with one of the roast shallots, a pinch of salt and pepper and 2 tsp of the finished stock to moisten the mix. Blend, then decant the pâté with a rubber spatula into a bowl and reserve.

Reduce the partridge stock to a rich concentrated glaze (about one-quarter of the original volume). Taste the reduced stock, and remember as the liquid reduces, so the concentration of the salts increases, so *don't* add any extra seasoning unless you are sure it is absolutely necessary.

Blanch the Savoy cabbage in boiling water for 1 minute, drain and set aside.

To assemble the dish, reheat the cabbage with the remaining butter and a spoonful of partridge stock, and place a bed in the centre of each heated dinner plate. The partridge breasts should be lightly brushed with olive oil, seasoned with salt and pepper and pan-fried in the metal-handled pan with the remaining garlic cloves, skin-side down for 2–3 minutes to seal the meat and crisp the skin. Then turn each fillet over, remove the garlic cloves, add a dash of cognac to deglaze the pan and place the pan in the hot oven. About 5 minutes should be enough for small breasts – but check as not all domestic ovens operate at the temperatures they claim.

Meanwhile, fry the bread triangles in a little more oil

until golden-brown. Drain well on kitchen paper.

When the partridge is ready (test the bottom side of each breast with a sharp skewer to check it is medium rare), place on the bed of cabbage and dress each breast liberally with the game glaze. Spread each crouton triangle with pâté and arrange on each side. Serve with the carrot purée and Lyonnaise-style potatoes.

DESSERT 27

Amaretti rum truffle cake with a raspberry coulis

1 tsp hazelnut oil
5 × 150 g (5 oz) bars luxury dark continental
    chocolate (75% cocoa solids)
1.2 litres (2 pints) fresh double cream
25 g (1 oz) icing sugar
2 tbsp liquid glucose
150 ml (¼ pint) dark Caribbean rum
1 box (about 20 pieces) Amaretti biscuits

  Raspberry coulis
4 small punnets fresh raspberries
juice of 1 lemon
a dash of crème de cassis
caster sugar

Cake method

You will need a 25 cm (10 in) springform tin and some greaseproof or baking parchment. Fit the tin together and oil the sides and bottom with the hazelnut oil using kitchen paper. Cut a disc of greaseproof

or baking parchment to fit the base and a collar to line the sides, protruding 5 mm (¼ in) above the top edge of the tin.

Break the chocolate into small chunks and melt in a small bowl above boiling water, ensuring the bottom of the bowl does not touch the surface of the water, otherwise the chocolate will congeal and harden.

Whisk the double cream with the icing sugar until it forms a stiff mass, and then add the glucose and rum and whisk again.

Crumble the biscuits finely, and sprinkle half onto the bottom surface of the tin, adding the other half to the cream. Then rapidly stir the warm melted chocolate into the cream, blending the mix quickly and thoroughly to ensure the chocolate is finely blended together without chunks forming. The mix will tend to set quickly, so work fast. Pour the chocolate mix into the lined tin and tap gently into the corners. With a palette knife or spatula, smooth over the top of the tin to make a flat surface.

Rest the dessert in the fridge for a couple of hours to allow it to set. Serve by uncoupling the tin side, inverting the cake on to a flat plate, and peeling off the paper sides. Cut into thin sections with a warm knife that has been dipped into hot water, and serve with the raspberry coulis.

Coulis method

Simply place the raspberries, lemon juice and cassis into a blender and process at a medium speed for a few seconds to pulp the fruits. Taste the coulis, adding a sprinkle or two of caster sugar if needed. You should remember that the fruit sauce must have a tart flavour to balance the heavy sweetness of the cake. Sieve if you like to get rid of the seeds.

Queen scallops on a broad bean purée with a red pepper and chilli coulis

Broad bean purée

900 g (2 lb) podded broad beans, shelled weight
80 g (3 oz) shallots, peeled and finely chopped
3 tbsp olive oil
3 garlic cloves, peeled and crushed
400 ml (14 fl oz) white wine
400 ml (14 fl oz) double cream
sea salt and freshly ground black pepper

Red pepper and chilli coulis

8 red peppers
3 fresh red chillies
25 g (1 oz) butter
sea salt and freshly ground black pepper

Scallops

64 queen scallops if smallish, otherwise 56 larger
    ones, wrapped in smoked streaky bacon
    (you'll need about 675 g 1½ lb) *
4 tbsp olive oil
chopped chervil

Take the rind off the bacon, and stretch each rasher to flatten and lengthen. If the scallops are small you may be able to get three to a rasher.

Bean purée method

Blanch the beans for 2 minutes, then refresh in cold water and remove the skins.*

Do not attempt to skip this part of the preparation. The skins are bitter and will ruin the purée if left in.

Sweat the shallots in the olive oil for 3 minutes on a medium flame, then add the garlic and cook on for 2 more minutes. Add the broad beans and wine and reduce the liquid by half. Next, add the cream and continue to reduce until the cream coats the beans.

Now divide the bean mixture into two. Put one half into a processor and pulse-chop roughly. Decant and reserve. Mouli the other half on a fine sieve, then combine the two together, warm through and adjust the seasonings.

Coulis method

Roast the peppers and chillies either in a very hot oven, or over a flame or char-grill to blister the skin and then sweat under a clingfilmed bowl (see page 43). When cool enough to handle, peel the skins off both peppers and chillies and de-seed and core them. Process on high speed to purée them, then reduce on a slow simmer in a saucepan until they thicken up. Stir in the butter, and adjust seasonings.

To cook and serve

Preheat the oven to 180°C/350°F/Gas 4.

Pan-fry the scallops in the olive oil to a golden-brown colour, then cook on in the medium hot oven for a couple of minutes.

Arrange the finished scallops on a bed of broad bean purée, and spoon the red pepper coulis around the outside. Scatter finely chopped chervil over the whole dish.

Roast beef with celeriac and potato mash and Yorkshire pudding

Suggested accompaniments
Creamed beetroot (see page 143)
Roast potatoes (see page 150)

Most people we know enjoy roast beef properly done. The beauty of roasting a rib joint is twofold. Firstly, the quality of texture and taste is the best, and secondly, as the ribs diminish in size along the rack of ribs the meat emerges with differing degrees of rareness – the biggest end producing the rarest and the smaller end giving a more medium result. Thus all tastes are catered for, and it is almost impossible to find meat left over.

Here we give portions which allow for seconds, and inject an element of what we call 'beef frenzy' – sheer wanton lust for eating flesh which is crispy on the outside and juicy in the middle. Ask the butcher to chine the bone, that is, to partially sever the chine end of the chop bone, which will allow heat to enter from the thickest end of the joint and ensure even cooking.

The celeriac and potato combo with vanilla makes an interesting departure from the traditional roast potatoes, but we give you our recipe for those as well, just in case. The creamed beetroot is spectacular with beef, and Yorkshire pudding is an unbeatable accompaniment. To complete the dish a green leafy vegetable is good: English cabbage will balance the purée with a crunchy texture.

1 rib joint of British beef, about 5 ribs' width,
*about 6.75 kg (15 lb) wet weight ***

4 tbsp olive oil
sea salt and ground white pepper
1 large Spanish onion, peeled and thickly sliced
2 small carrots, thickly sliced
½ bottle robust red wine

Celeriac and potato mash
3 large heads celeriac
1.4 kg (3 lb) potatoes (Maris Piper)
light chicken stock (see page 155)
175–250 ml (6–8 fl oz) extra-virgin olive oil
freshly ground black pepper/horseradish sauce
4 tsp fresh vanilla extract (Madagascan is good),
to taste

* *For the meat to be well presented, it is important to allow the joint to rise to room temperature. This will take at least an hour from a standard fridge.*

Meat method 1

Rub the surface of the joint with a little olive oil and sprinkle with white pepper and salt, rubbing it well into the crevices. Place in a roasting tin on top of the onion and carrot (which act as a trivet), and pour into the bottom of the tin the red wine. (You can drink the other half as you proceed further. It is a most enjoyable way to get the meal ready.)

Next, the meat must be roasted in a very hot (230°C/450°F/Gas 8) oven for 20 minutes to seal it. Then, the temperature can be reduced to hot (200–220°C/400–425°F/Gas 6–7) for the rest of the cooking time. If you allow 20 minutes per 450g (1 lb), this should give you a rough guide, for a range within the joint from rare to medium/well done on the ends.*

* *Important note for conventional or for convecting ovens. A rib of beef this size is about the biggest object you'll probably ever put in your oven. Halfway through the cooking time, it is a good idea to rotate the meat so that the heat absorbed will be even. Fan ovens are supposed to roast evenly, but huge*

pieces of beef impede air flow around the oven – so be warned.

Celeriac and potato mash method

Meanwhile, prepare the celeriac by peeling thickly to remove 'eyes'. Peel the potatoes as well, and cut both into chunks. Cook until tender in stock to cover. Drain and mouli the mash together in the usual way (see page 147), then add the olive oil (instead of the more usual butter), adjusting seasoning as necessary. When combined, add the vanilla essence and stir throughout. Set aside to await the meat.

To reheat, simply stir around slowly on a low flame, ensuring the mixture does not catch and stick. Before serving, check for vanilla flavour. Vanilla is a volatile essence and may lose some of its potency while standing, so add more, if necessary.

Meat method 2

When the meat is ready (a judicious prod of the end surfaces will show how well-done it is, and a meat thermometer is also a useful guide), take it out to rest under a sheet of kitchen foil for at least 15 minutes. This will give you time to prepare the gravy and allow the fibres of the beef to loosen and become set for carving.

Gravy is easily made by reducing the meat juices and wine on the top of the hob, then straining them through a fine wire sieve, and adjusting for seasoning. Add a little stock to give a savoury addition (not too much as the celery taste must not dominate the meaty flavours). It is important, too, not to have added a lot of salt to the original meat surface – remember, reduction increases all the flavours, including salt, so don't overdo it.

Carving should be done onto warm plates – the rarest slices coming from the middle of the large end.

Yorkshire pudding

We make our own dripping for this by slicing a thin layer of fat from the side of the meat and rendering it down. Batter poured into the hot dripping will produce the best results. Batter poured into a cold or lukewarm tin will never rise properly.

> *110 g (4 oz) self-raising flour*
> *a large pinch of salt*
> *300 ml (½ pint) whole milk*
> *1 large egg (or 2 small), lightly beaten*
> *1 tbsp melted butter*
> *4 tbsp melted beef dripping*

Method

Sift the flour and salt into a mixing bowl and beat to a smooth texture with half the milk plus the beaten eggs and the melted butter. Stir in the remaining milk, and whisk together well. Leave for 15 minutes to allow the glutens to emerge. This will ensure a better result.

About 35 minutes before the meat is to be taken out, place the beef dripping in the oven in a large 25 × 30 cm (10 × 12 in) baking tray. Allow to heat for 4–5 minutes until smoking and then pour in the batter.* Place in the top of the oven for 10–15 minutes, then on the bottom for another 15 minutes. Finally, when the meat is removed, place the tin in the middle to finish and crisp up around the edges. The initial heat raises the batter, the bottom cooking cooks it right through, and the final browning avoids a soggy middle. Good luck, and remember, a hot start is the key to success.

* The depth of the batter in the tray should be no more than 1 cm (½ in).

DESSERT 28

Baked apple with brown sugar and spices

Baked apple may sound a bit like school dinners, but trust us, it's darn good. It can be made a little more special with a good chilled dessert wine. This dish also follows a cheese course well.

8 dried apricots, chopped
50 g (2 oz) raisins
50 g (2 oz) sultanas
25 g (1 oz) shelled almonds, chopped
2 tbsp rum
zest and juice of 1 lemon
zest and juice of 1 orange
8 large Bramley cooking apples
4 tbsp demerara sugar
½ tsp powdered cinnamon
¼ tsp ground allspice
2 tbsp unsalted butter
2 tbsp golden syrup
double cream

Method

Macerate the apricots and other dried fruits with the almonds in the rum and the citrus zests and juice for 1 hour.

Meanwhile, core the apples with a circular corer, vertically, and score a horizontal line through the skin of each apple around the 'equator'. (This will prevent the apple splitting randomly during baking.)

Heat the oven to 220°C/425°F/Gas 7.

After the maceration time, add the sugar and spices to the fruit filling, mix together and fill the holes in each apple. Arrange them in a roasting dish, put a good knob of butter on top of each one, and pour the golden syrup lightly over each apple to cover the skin. Pour 8 tbsp of water into the dish to prevent sticking and dot any remaining butter in and around the dish. Bake for 30–40 minutes. The apples should be cooked perfectly throughout but not falling apart and turning into jam. To help the process, baste occasionally with the pan juices, which will reduce slightly during cooking into a syrup.

To serve, place each apple on a warmed dessert plate and pour over the syrup. This is quite a rich dish, so double cream will be sufficient to accompany it.

STARTER 29

Black squid ink linguine with prawns, chilli and garlic

150 ml (¼ pint) olive oil
675 g (1½ lb) fresh green king prawns, cleaned,
*   peeled and shelled, head off*
sea salt and freshly ground black pepper
4 garlic cloves, peeled and sliced thinly
3 small red chillies, de-seeded and finely sliced
800 g (1¾ lb) linguine nero (black squid ink
*   pasta)*

Method

Heat the oil to hot and fry the prawns, seasoning

them as they are being cooked, for 2–3 minutes to just colour them up. Stir in the garlic and chillies.

Cook the black linguine in salted boiling water until al dente, then drain well and toss in the oil and garlic sauce. This is supposed to be a rich dish so don't worry about the high density of olive oil, it's deliberate.

MAIN COURSE 29

Grilled lobster with lime and oregano butter and a green seafood sauce

Green seafood sauce
2 slices white bread, crusts removed
10 tbsp white vinegar
8 tbsp extra-virgin olive oil
8 tbsp chopped parsley (flat-leaf preferred)
4 garlic cloves, peeled and chopped
6 anchovy fillets, finely chopped
2 tsp caster sugar
3 tsp drained capers

Seasoned butter
90 g (3½ oz) slightly salted butter
2 tbsp olive oil
2 tbsp freshly squeezed lime juice
1 tbsp finely chopped fresh oregano

Lobsters
4 Scottish lobsters
corn oil
sea salt

Seafood sauce method

Tear the bread into pieces and place in a bowl with 6 tbsp vinegar and soak until the bread is saturated, about 30 minutes. Place into a blender/mixer machine, and add the olive oil, parsley, garlic, anchovies and sugar. Process until well mixed. Add the capers and the remaining vinegar. Let the sauce stand for at least half an hour for the flavours to blend and then chill.

For serving, the sauce must be left at room temperature for at least 1 hour to let the ambient heat in the room bring back the flavours.

Butter method

Melt the butter, combine with the olive oil, and beat in the lime juice and oregano. Remove from the heat and let the sauce stand for 1 hour for the flavours to develop.

Lobster method

Slightly under-cook the lobsters in boiling highly salted water (to mimic sea water) – about 4 minutes per 450 g (1 lb). Halve lengthways, then clean out the intestinal cavity near the head, discarding contents.

Brush the grill with corn oil to prevent sticking, and preheat. Grill each half lobster cut-side to the heat first, and then shell-side to the heat. The flesh exposed can then be brushed with the seasoned butter and sprinkled with salt *without* the flare-up and smoke.

To serve

Serve the half lobster, spooning the seafood sauce into the convenient space alongside the flesh.

Nosh rich rum cake

1 recipe sablé *pastry (see page 59)*
225 g (8 oz) cocoa powder, sifted
110 g (4 oz) caster sugar
2 large eggs, beaten
225 g (8 oz) cocoa butter, warmed
120 ml (4 fl oz) dark strong rum

Method

Preheat the oven to 200°C/400°F/Gas 6.

Make the 'biscuit' first. Roll out sheets of the pastry very thinly to cover baking trays (when it rises, you want a layer no more than 1 cm / ½ in thick), then bake in the oven for 15–20 minutes – they should be very pale. Leave to cool, then cut to size.*

* The biscuit layers should fit the tin exactly, so if your tin has sloping sides, cut even wider strips.

Mix the cocoa powder, sugar and eggs together, then add the cocoa butter a little at a time. When combined and smooth, gradually add the rum.

To construct the cake, line a long loaf tin, about 10 cm (4 in) high, with foil, leaving spare foil flaps to overlap. Spread a layer of choccy mix evenly over the base *and sides* to a thickness of about 1 cm (½ in). Then place a layer of biscuit (which should be no more than 5 mm / ¼ in thick) tightly over the choc layer. Top this with another layer of choc mix, but this time only 5 mm (¼ in) thick. Carry on layering until the tin is nearly full – then finish with a choc mix layer of 1 cm (½ in) thickness. Then, fold over the foil flaps to seal the cake tightly, wrap in clingfilm and refrigerate for two to three days before opening.

To serve, unwrap carefully and then thinly slice across the grain. As this is a very rich recipe, it should be sliced *sparingly*. (Remember to wrap the cake up tightly again afterwards, to keep the cake moist.)

STARTER 30

Wild mushroom soup

500 g (18 oz) closed cup field mushrooms
300 g (10 oz) selection of wild mushrooms *
1 large Spanish (mild) onion, peeled and very
  finely chopped
1 tbsp olive oil
80 g (3 oz) unsalted butter
1 garlic clove, peeled and crushed
1.4 litres (2½ pints) chicken stock (see page 155)
300 ml (½ pint) whole milk
sea salt and freshly ground black pepper
½ tsp freshly grated nutmeg
300 ml (½ pint) single cream
4 tbsp chopped fresh parsley

* Try to choose, if possible, varieties that will not discolour the soup (i.e. no amethyst deceiver, black trompettes, etc., but plenty of light-coloured fungi such as girolles, ceps, chanterelles, etc.).

Method

Clean the fungi with a pastry brush (rinse if necessary), and allow to drain. Chop all the fungi, except 110 g (4 oz) of the wild selection, reserving this for the garnish. (These can be sweated off separately in a little olive oil and, when tender, allowed to cool.)

Sweat the onion in the olive oil and butter in a large saucepan for 6 minutes on a low to medium flame, stirring to prevent catching and sticking. You should achieve a light golden transparent colour. Add the mushrooms and garlic and sauté along with the onions on a high heat. The juices released by the mushrooms will prevent the onions over-colouring. Add the chicken stock when the juices are starting to dry up, and cook for 10 minutes on a slow simmer. Then add the milk, bring back to the boil and simmer for another 5 minutes. Adjust the seasoning, with salt, pepper and nutmeg, and whizz the whole lot through a processor until the soup has a smooth to medium texture. It should be able to be spooned easily but not so smooth that it resembles baby food.

Serve in warmed bowls with a swirl of fresh single cream and a spoonful of the reserved fried wild mushrooms in the centre for garnish. A light sprinkling of finely chopped parsley will complete the soup.

MAIN COURSE 30

Breast of pheasant with orange and port

Suggested accompaniments
Celeriac and carrot purée (see page 143)

4 medium pheasants
175 ml (6 fl oz) veal stock (see page 155)
300 ml (½ pint) chicken stock (see page 155)
90 ml (3 fl oz) port
juice of 1 orange
zest of ½ orange
sea salt and freshly ground black pepper

4 large streaky bacon rashers
2 tsp redcurrant jelly

Method

Using a very sharp knife, cut the breasts (with skin) from each carcass and set aside. Chop each carcass into small pieces and roast in a hot oven (220°C/ 425°F/Gas 7) for 15 minutes. Then place the bones into a large saucepan with the veal and chicken stocks, along with the port and orange juice. Boil to reduce by two-thirds in volume, to make a very rich dense stock. Add the zest. Allow to cool for 15 minutes, and then reserve after sieving, discarding all bones and bits.

Season each breast lightly and lay a half piece of streaky bacon over each. This will prevent the lean meat from drying out. Roast the breasts in a reduced oven (200°C/400°F/Gas 6) in a 5 mm (¼ in) layer of the reduced stock (to prevent the bottom burning) for about 25–35 minutes or more, depending on size and desired degree of rareness. Then lift the breasts out and keep warm. Place the roasting pan on top of the hob and stir the meat juices and residue around, adding the remaining reduced stock and the redcurrant jelly. Serve this poured over the breasts on individual hot plates.

DESSERT 30

Pears poached in Beaumes de Venise

8 large ripe, firm Comice (or similar) pears
½ bottle Beaumes de Venise dessert wine
1 small stick cinnamon
clotted cream

Method

Peel and quarter the pears and remove the cores. Place in a saucepan with the dessert wine and cinnamon and bring to the boil slowly. Then simmer for 5 minutes or so until the pears are tender. Remove the cinnamon and discard it, then take out the pears and set aside.

To make the sauce, reduce the wine on a high heat until it has a syrupy texture. Place the pears back in the pan, and let cool until you're able to refrigerate.

Serve chilled with clotted cream.

STARTER 31

Soto ayam Madura

In Indonesia, where this recipe comes from, there are as many versions of chicken soup as islands – and there are about 17,000 of the latter! This is Mick's favourite, from the island of Madura, and is so good, you never get bored with eating it. Madura is famous also for the amorous qualities of its local women – who are considered the spiciest items of the South-East Asian smorgasbord!

1 premier-quality chicken, about 1.1 kg (2½ lb),
*   or thighs and legs*
150 g (5 oz) small green prawns, peeled, de-veined
*   and coarsely chopped*
1.75 litres (3 pints) water
1 soft inner core lemongrass, cut into small pieces
3 kaffir lime leaves *
4 small eggs, hard-boiled, peeled and halved

110 g (4 oz) glass noodles (mung bean vermicelli),
   pre-soaked in cold water
110 g (4 oz) beansprouts
3 largish potatoes, peeled, boiled and thinly sliced
a small handful of white cabbage, finely shredded
   and blanched for 10 seconds until it wilts
8 spinach leaves, blanched for 10 seconds until
   they wilt
salt and freshly ground black pepper
2 tbsp fresh lime juice

   Spice paste
8 small shallots, peeled and roughly chopped
10 small garlic cloves, peeled
1 × 2.5 cm (1 in) piece fresh ginger, peeled and
   roughly chopped
a pinch of ground tumeric
4 Macadamia nuts, roasted and finely ground
½ tsp roasted cumin seeds
1 tbsp peanut oil

* Kaffir lime leaves are the leaves of the largish warty
limes (sometimes called 'wild limes') seen in Asian
food stores. The fruits are not particularly juicy but
the leaves (which occur as two on a single central
stem) are valuable in South-East Asian cooking. They
are usually bought fresh in plastic bags. Dried, they
lose a lot of character and we would not recommend
using them.

Method

If using a whole chicken, joint it. Put into a large
saucepan with the prawns, the water, lemongrass and
lime leaves. Bring to the boil on a high heat, skim off
any froth or scummy residue, and then turn down to
a slow simmer.

In a blender, process together the spice paste ingredients except for the oil, then fry in the peanut oil for
a few minutes until the flavours have blended and it
has a strong cooked aroma. Mix this with about 250
ml (8 fl oz) water to thoroughly dissolve, then add to

the pot with the chicken. Simmer on for about 45
minutes, or until the chicken is tender. Remove the
meat, reserving the broth, and cut the chicken meat
into shreds, discarding the bones.

To serve

Everyone should have individual bowls between
which are divided the cooked chicken, egg halves,
noodles and vegetables with a generous ladling of
seasoned broth. Any extra hotness can be adjusted
by the addition of *sambal* (a hot chutney), as below.
The soup can be topped off with chopped celery
leaves, chopped spring onions and a squeeze of lime
juice. In addition, brown crispy fried onions make a
great garnish.

Indonesians often create a lunch for themselves by
serving this soup with a side dish of rice on a separate plate and then spooning the soup and chicken
on to it as they eat, alternating between the two.

Sambal soto

This is a hot condiment for Madura chicken soup.

   6 macadamia nuts, roasted
   8 fresh red chillies, cored and de-seeded
   ½ tsp shrimp paste, toasted on a sheet of foil *
   2 tbsp kecup manis (Javanese sweet soy sauce)
   sea salt

* Toasting the shrimp paste seems laborious, but will
transform the flavour, allowing maximum pungency
to develop.

Method

Grind all the ingredients together in a blender and
moisten with a little water to create a wet paste. Small
dabs of this condiment can be stirred into the soup
if a hotter taste is required.

Roast suckling pig with coconut rice

For this you will need your largest roasting tray.

1 suckling pig, about 2 kg (4½ lb), cleaned
    and boned *
sea salt
lemon juice
2 small oranges

Marinade

3 tbsp peanut oil
1 tsp Chinese five-spice powder
1 tbsp coconut-palm sugar
2 tbsp dark soy sauce
1 tbsp Asian fish sauce
½ tsp freshly ground black pepper
6 garlic cloves, peeled and crushed
1 tbsp finely chopped fresh ginger
2 tbsp strong-flavoured honey

If you ask the butcher, he will bone out the cavity for you, but get him to leave the leg bones in for rigidity and appearance. This means that when carved, the slices through the back will be entirely lean, without any attached ribs.

Method

Wash out the gutted body cavity* with cold fresh water and pat dry inside with a clean tea towel.

When boned, the pork will tend to sag and lose its cylindrical shape – just put a couple of small oranges into the body to keep the shape or, if you have time, the cavity can be stuffed with a suitable cooked rice (like the coconut rice below) and even sewn up with butcher's string.

With a very sharp knife, score the surface skin lightly (exactly as if preparing crackling on a Sunday roast). Mix all the marinade ingredients together, and smear over the piggy. Leave in the marinade in a large dish for at least a few hours, and preferably overnight.

For roasting, preheat the oven to 200°C/400°F/ Gas 6. Salt the pork inside and out, then place in a roasting dish (on a wire roasting rack is good). Allow to roast until done, with the crackling crispy, which will take about ¾–1 hour, depending on the weight of the beast. But keep an eye on its progress. You may have to baste frequently and increase the oven setting slightly if the crackling is not crisping.*

About halfway through the cooking time, squeeze some lemon juice on to the outside surface of the pork – this will help the crackling to crisp up.

Coconut rice

Coconut rice is served at festive occasions in Indonesia , such as a wedding feast. It is very simple to cook.

550 g (1¼ lb) short grain white rice
475 ml (16 fl oz) coconut milk
1 small carton coconut cream – about 150 ml
    (¼ pint)
2 pandanus leaves *
sea salt to taste

Pandanus leaves are unique to South-East Asian cooking and are also known as screwpine leaves. They contribute colour and fragrance, and are obtainable from good oriental supermarkets as fresh raw leaves or essence. To cook with rice, tie the leaves together into a knot and chuck into the cooking rice. Remove and discard before eating.

Method

Wash the rice well in a strainer or colander until the water runs clear. Drain. Place the rice in a saucepan, preferably heavy-based, with the coconut milk and cream, the pandanus leaves and salt. Bring to the boil and then simmer, covered, for about 20 minutes until all the liquid has been absorbed. Remove the pan from the heat, and place a clean tea towel (no contaminating fabric conditioners please!) under the lid. Allow the rice to steam in its own heat for 20 minutes. This will allow it to dry somewhat.

DESSERT 31

Guava cheesecake

To fill two 20 cm (8 in) round pie dishes.

Guava purée
4 large guavas, weighing about 150 g (5 oz) each,
*   peeled, washed and roughly chopped*
4 tbsp caster sugar
2 tbsp lemon juice
9 tbsp cold water

Guava jelly
1 × 45 g (½ oz) sachet powdered gelatine
450 ml (¾ pint) water
8 tbsp caster sugar
4 tbsp lemon juice
half the guava purée (above)

Cheesecake mixture
1 × 45 g (1½ oz) sachet powdered gelatine
5 tbsp cold water
900 g (2 lb) mascarpone cream cheese

half the guava purée (above)
75 g (6 oz) creamy Greek yogurt

Guava purée method

Put the guavas in a saucepan, add the rest of the purée ingredients, and cook on a slow heat, stirring occasionally, for 30 minutes. Transfer the mixture to a blender and whizz until smooth. Then pass it through a fine sieve into a bowl. Divide the purée into two equal portions.

Guava jelly method

Put the gelatine in a small saucepan and add 5 tbsp of the water. Leave aside until all the water has been absorbed. In another, bigger, saucepan, bring the rest of the water and the sugar to the boil. Let it bubble for 3 minutes, and stir to ensure the sugar has dissolved. Add the half of the guava purée, stir again and simmer for 2 minutes. Meanwhile heat the smaller saucepan with the 'liquid' gelatine in it and, when completely melted, stir into the guava mixture. Cool and pour into a serving dish. Refrigerate until it begins to set.

Cheesecake method

Put the gelatine in a small saucepan with the water and leave as before to absorb, ready for melting. Put the rest of the cheesecake ingredients in a blender and blend for a few seconds. Heat the saucepan with the gelatine until melted, then stir into the guava and cheese mixture. Blend again for a few seconds.

By now the cooling guava jelly will have started to set. Take it out of the fridge, and pour the cheese and guava mixture carefully on top. Level the cheese and guava with the back of a spoon and return it to the fridge for at least 4 hours, preferably overnight.

To serve

To serve, cut with a large knife that has been wetted

with hot water. Lift each slice out of the dish with a cake slice or spatula.

Pan-fried foie gras with balsamic vinegar on toasted brioche

900 g (2 lb) fresh goose or duck foie gras
1 small brioche loaf
olive oil
sea salt and freshly ground black pepper
2 tsp good-quality balsamic vinegar

Method

Gently separate the lobes of the foie gras and clean of all membranes, skin and any small threads of veins or nerve tissue. Soak the liver in water overnight, then clean it and pat dry with kitchen paper. As foie gras is an 'enriched' offal, it shrinks somewhat due to the fats being 'cooked out', so slice off sections weighing about 60 g (2 oz) each. This will give two pieces per starter portion.

Brush each slice of brioche very lightly with olive oil, and toast under a hot grill until slightly light brown, then keep warm.

To pan-fry the liver, preheat a large frying pan to medium hot and put a thin brushing of olive oil in. (Do not *over*-heat the pan otherwise the oil will smoke and the liver burn. Season each slice of foie gras with salt and pepper and pan-fry until some of the fatty juices melt and escape and the slices take on patches of colour. Turn over and cook the other side (about 1 minute on each side will be enough). Halfway through the second side, splash in the balsamic vinegar to deglaze the pan. The tartness will balance the richness of the foie gras.

To serve, place each slice of foie gras on a slice of brioche at a slant, and dress with a little freshly ground black pepper.

Fillet steak marinated in black bean and teriyaki sauce

8 × 175 g (6 oz) Scotch beef fillet steaks, larder trimmed *
3 tbsp black bean sauce (for marinade, not stir-fry)
6 tbsp off-the-shelf teriyaki sauce (e.g. Kikkoman)
3 garlic cloves, peeled and crushed into 120 ml (4 fl oz) olive oil
1 oakleaf lettuce
3 small punnets lamb's lettuce
honey dressing (see page 37)
2 ciabatta loaves

* Larder-trimmed means chain (the long sinewy strip that runs along the length of the whole fillet) and all fat and sinews removed. British beef, especially Scottish fillet, remains one of our favourites.

Method

Flatten each steak, end grain up, with a meat mallet or rolling pin until it is no thicker than 8 mm (⅓ in). Next mix together the black bean and teriyaki sauces and the garlic oil. Dip each thin slice of fillet into the marinade and let rest for 15 minutes.*

* Note that 15 minutes is enough for this marinade. Too long and the salty nature will draw out the beef juices and render it rather dry.

Meanwhile, prepare the side salad. Dress with honey dressing just before serving, tossing it in a large bowl. Cut each ciabatta loaf into four pieces, split open and toast each piece ready for serving.

To cook the beef, set the grill on very hot (char-grilling is also a great alternative) and grill each slice for about 1 minute on each side. This should give a pinkness to the centre.* Place on a piece of toasted ciabatta, and serve with the freshly dressed side salad.

* Ensure that the fillet is not over-grilled – fillet has little or no marbling within it and will dry out if not watched carefully.

DESSERT 32

Pont-l'Évêque, Camembert and mustard fruits

1 Pont-l'Évêque cheese (unpasteurized if
    possible)
1 unpasteurized Camembert
675 g (1½ lb) mostarda di frutta (see below)

Mostarda di frutta (mustard fruits) *

200 g (7 oz) caster sugar
about 2 litres (3½ pints) water (to cover fruits)
120 ml (4 fl oz) lemon juice
450 g (1 lb) quinces or pears
225 g (8 oz) rhubarb or apple
450 g (1 lb) fresh peaches
225 g (8 oz) fresh apricots
225 g (8 oz) plums
3 tbsp yellow mustard seeds
1 lemon, sliced into rounds
5–6 slices peeled fresh ginger
6 cloves
250 ml (8 fl oz) dry white wine
225 g (8 oz) honey

* Makes about 2.3 litres / 4 pints, which is more than you need for this recipe, but it can be bottled for future use.

Method

To make the pickled fruits, combine the sugar, water and lemon juice in a heavy-based pan. Boil and then simmer to dissolve the sugar, stirring frequently (about 5 minutes).

Add the firmest fruit first – the quinces or pears, and apple if using – and simmer for 10 minutes. Then add the softer fruits and continue to simmer for a few more minutes, but don't let the fruit go mushy! Remove the fruit with a slotted spoon. Reserve the syrup. Dry the fruit in a large tray in a warm oven (140–150°C/275–300°F/Gas 1–2) for about 3 hours and then leave to get cold.

Soak the mustard seeds in water for 10 minutes, then drain. Add to the syrup with the lemon, ginger and cloves in a muslin bag. Add the wine and honey and boil to reduce until it's very thick. Place the dried fruits in sterile jars, pour over the reduced syrup, and store in a cool place.

Goose liver terrine 'foie gras' style

You can get foie gras livers which are from ducks, but a goose foie gras gives the richest results. This terrine should be started at least five days before serving (but can keep up to two weeks after it's ready).

You will need a glazed earthenware terrine dish or rectangular pâté tin, a good board to fit it, and a 900g (2lb) weight.

1 goose foie gras liver (up to 2 kg/4½ lb)
50 g (2 oz) black truffles (peeled weight)
a pinch of quatre-épices *
sea salt, ground white pepper and freshly ground
   black pepper
600 ml (1 pint) Armagnac/port (50:50 mix) for
   the marinade
1 tbsp goose fat for greasing
about 8 thin slices of Carpegna Italian
   prosciutto
110g (4oz) unsalted butter for sealing

   Stuffing
300 g (10 oz) lean pork, minced
300 g (10 oz) lean veal, minced
50 g (2 oz) smoked streaky bacon, minced
3 chicken livers, sautéed rare in a little butter
2 eggs
50 g (2 oz) fresh whitebreadcrumbs
3 tbsp Armagnac
a pinch of herbes de Provence

* Quatre-épices – *literally 'four spices' – is a season-ing combo that originated in classic French cuisine. A similar mix also had a vogue in English cooking in Tudor times. It is equal quantities of ground nutmeg, cayenne pepper, allspice and mace.*

Method

Gently separate the lobes of the foie gras and clean free of all membranes, skin, and any small threads of veins or nerve tissue. Soak the liver in water overnight, then clean it and pat dry with kitchen paper.

Cut the truffles into wedges.

Mix the *quatre-épices* with a little salt, white and black pepper. Make several cuts into the lobes, sprin-kle a pinch of spice into each and then insert a wedge of truffle into each slit. Next, put the liver into a bowl and cover with the Armagnac and port mix for 4 hours.

Meanwhile, mix all the stuffing ingredients together. Add 4 tbsp of the Armagnac/port marinade. The breadcrumbs will soak up any slack moisture.

Grease the terrine dish or pâté tin on the sides and bottom with goose fat, then line with the prosciutto. Traditional recipes call for barding fat to seal the ter-rine, but this can make the result very oily. Carpegna ham is very sweet and has enough refined fat on each slice to keep the terrine moist.

Next, fill the terrine one-third full with the stuffing, leaving a channel along the length into which to fit the lobes of the foie gras. Cover with the remainder of the stuffing, then smooth off the surface with a palette knife dipped into warm water. Place a layer of prosciutto snugly over the surface and cover with foil.

Cook in a bain-marie in a medium hot oven (160–180°C/325–350°F/Gas 3–4) for 1 hour or until the juices that run out appear clear, when the foil is peeled back for inspection.

Put a thick piece of board – cut to fit the top rectangle exactly – on top and leave overnight to cool with a 900 g (2 lb) weight on top.

Next day, peel away the foil and pour over a thin layer of melted clarified butter to seal it. When cool, re-seal with fresh foil and store for three days in the coolest part of the fridge to allow the flavours to develop.

MAIN COURSE 33

Beef fillet parcels with mushrooms and cognac

Suggested accompaniments
Caramelized carrots (see page 143)
Sauté potatoes (see page 146)

A variation on the classic beef Wellington, we have adapted it by making each portion in an individual crust and replacing the traditional liver pâté with a mushroom pâté.

8 × 225 g (8 oz) best-quality Scotch beef fillet
steaks, larder-trimmed *
olive oil
sea salt and ground white pepper
50 g (2 oz) clarified unsalted butter
2 tbsp cognac
freshly ground black pepper
fresh puff pastry, 8 sheets, 25 cm (10 in)
square
eggwash for brushing pastry **

Mushroom pâté
225 g (8 oz) mixed wild mushrooms
2 tbsp good-quality olive oil
2 shallots, peeled
1 garlic clove, peeled and crushed

sea salt and freshly ground black pepper
2 tbsp chopped parsley

* Larder-trimmed means chain (the long sinewy strip that runs along the length of the whole fillet) and all fat and sinews removed. British beef, especially Scottish fillet, remains one of our favourites.

** Eggwash is 1 egg yolk with 3 tbsp milk and a pinch of salt whisked together to be applied with a pastry brush to the edges (to seal) and to the top surface to achieve a golden-brown colour on baking.

Method

Press each fillet steak slightly flat with the palm of your hand so that it is 4 cm (1½ in) maximum thickness. Brush each steak on all sides with olive oil, then season with sea salt and ground white pepper. Set aside to reach room temperature while the mushroom pâté is prepared.

Clean and trim all the wild mushrooms, rinsing if necessary to remove chaff and grit. Drain and dry, then slice and sweat off in a frying pan with the olive oil, shallots and garlic. When the juices have come out and the fungi have cooked dry, remove from the pan and place in a food processor with a little salt and pepper and the parsley, and process on a medium speed on pulse to reduce to a coarse pâté. Check the seasoning and then decant into a bowl.

To cook the steaks, swirl the butter in a hot frying pan on a high flame and seal each steak for 30 seconds or so on all sides. Then pour a generous splash of cognac into the pan and flame off. Remove each steak, season again with freshly ground black pepper and spread the top with a 5 mm (¼ in) layer of the mushroom pâté. Wrap each finished steak in a square of puff pastry, sealing overlapping edges with eggwash, and tucking them underneath the parcel.

Bake the fillet parcels in a hot oven (220°C/425°F/Gas 7) for about 12–16 minutes until the pastry has risen and is a rich golden-brown colour. (This should achieve a medium rare result.) If you have not sealed the parcels firmly, juices will escape and dampen the outside of the pastry, preventing the browning process, and the bottom layer of pastry will be soggy.

DESSERT 33

Figs in spiced vanilla syrup

This recipe adapts a technique used for centuries in the Middle East to preserve a glut of fruits. It produces a gourmet conserve that is useful as a basis for an elegant dessert.

In choosing your figs, taste them first. They can be classed as 'sweetest', 'middling' or 'less sweet', depending on their type and degree of ripeness. You can use any of them, but you must adjust the amount of sugar used. Try to obtain fruits that are firm: this way they will remain whole during cooking.

We are indebted to Marie Hekimian for her inspiring help in this recipe.

900 g (2 lb) fresh figs, whole
675 g (1½ lb) caster sugar (450 g/1 lb for sweetest; 900 g/2 lb for the less sweet ones)
600 ml (1 pint) water
12 cloves
4 fresh vanilla pods
2 cinnamon sticks
juice of ½ lemon
blanched skinned almonds

Method

Wash, drain and dry the figs. Place, pointed end up, with all the remaining ingredients, apart from the almonds, in a large saucepan. Bring to the boil and simmer until the conserve is a caramel colour. After 15 minutes, check the sweetness level, and adjust with more sugar or lemon juice, as appropriate. Insert a whole almond into the open end of each fig and continue cooking, for a maximum of another 15 minutes. Test by dripping a few drops of the syrup on to a cold surface, then pressing it between your finger and thumb. If your fingers stick together, it's cooked!

Place the hot mixture into a large glass jar or other container, cool, and allow to rest in the fridge for three days. Ensure the figs are entirely covered by the syrup.

Serve the figs with ice cream, garnished with the syrup.

STARTER 34

Langoustine ravioli with a dry Martini and cream sauce

Langoustines are 'all mouth and no trousers' as far as yield goes. But the flesh is very delicate and sweet, so quite incomparable for taste in this dish. You can make the recipe cheaper by substituting all or part of the langoustines with prawns, but we don't recommend it. It loses all the subtlety of flavour. It would be as sacrilegious as making bread and butter pudding with margarine. Don't even think about it!

1.8 kg (4 lb) fresh langoustines
900 g (2 lb) fresh pasta, rolled thinly *
sea salt and freshly ground black pepper
semolina or polenta for dusting

Sauce
1 large Spanish onion, peeled and finely
   chopped
20 long 'banana' shallots, peeled and finely
   chopped
2 large celery stalks, finely chopped
4 star anise
1 red chilli, de-seeded and finely chopped
2 tbsp olive oil
½ bottle dry Martini/Noilly Prat vermouth
600 ml (1 pint) fish stock (see page 154)
600 ml (1 pint) single cream

* *If you cannot get fresh pasta (lasagne sheets, for instance), or don't have the time to make it, Chinese won-ton wrappers are a very good substitute, and can be bought easily from oriental supermarkets.*

Sauce method

Pick out the langoustine meat from the shells and reserve. Place the claws and shells in a large pan and sweat off with the onion, shallots, celery, anise and chilli in the olive oil over a medium heat for 5 minutes. Keep stirring the mix and don't let the shallots become brown. Deglaze with the vermouth and add the stock and cream. Bring just to the boil and reduce to a thick sauce. Pass the sauce through a fine conical sieve, check seasoning, and keep warm.

Ravioli method

Cut squares or rounds of fresh pasta, making the 'lid' slightly larger than the base, to allow for the filling. Fill the ravioli with the seasoned langoustine meat, dampening the edges with cold water to get them to

stick, and rest on a wooden tray on a bed of semolina or polenta powder to prevent them sticking together.

Boil the ravioli for 2 minutes in salted water on a rolling boil, drain and divide between warm plates. Pour over the sauce generously.

MAIN COURSE 34

Rare-roast medallions of ostrich fillet on sweet potato with roast garlic and wilted spinach

Roast garlic
32 garlic cloves, peeled
6 tbsp olive oil

Sweet potato
1.4 kg (3 lb) sweet potato
50 g (2 oz) butter
150 ml (¼ pint) single cream
sea salt

Ostrich
24 × 80 g (3 oz) medallions of ostrich fillet,
   trimmed
sea salt and ground white pepper
1 tbsp plain flour
4 large shallots, peeled and finely chopped
a dash of Armagnac
120 ml (4 fl oz) light veal stock (see page 155)

Wilted spinach
1.4 kg (3 lb) baby spinach
a few drops of sesame oil
sea salt and freshly ground black pepper
25 g (1 oz) butter

Roast garlic method

Roast the garlic cloves in a moderate oven (180°C/350°F/Gas 4) in the oil until they have become a light brown colour, about 15–20 minutes. Remove and cool. Decant the garlic oil, and heat in a frying pan over a medium hot flame, reserving the roast garlic for later.

Sweet potato method

Best results are with the orange-coloured type of sweet potato. Boil them with skins on in plenty of well-salted water. Drench with cold water after they are ready, then peel the skins off, removing any 'eyes' or root threadlets. Use a coarse-mesh mouli to get the mash sieved well with no lumps, but a good even texture. Add the butter and cream and don't be frightened to add plenty of sea salt.

Ostrich method

Brush each medallion lightly with the garlic oil, season with salt and white pepper and dust very lightly on each side with flour, shaking off any excess. Pan-fry in the oil with the shallots and turn over after 3 minutes or so (to give a medium rare result). Flame with Armagnac and deglaze the pan with the stock. Add the whole roasted garlic cloves and serve on a bed of mashed sweet potato, with the spinach and the garlic cloves arranged roughly around the outside.

Spinach method

De-stem the spinach leaves and wash in plenty of cold water to remove any grit. Drain off the excess water. Stir-fry in a hot wok with only about 1 tsp oil, turning swiftly to prevent burning. There will be enough liquid clinging to the leaves and 'released' from the cooking process to help wilt the leaves. Season with salt and black pepper, drain any excess liquid from the wok, and swirl around the butter to give the spinach a shine. Serve immediately.

DESSERT 34

Mini-Pavlova meringues with clotted cream and passionfruit

a pinch of salt
7 egg whites
350 g (12 oz) caster sugar
1½ tsp cornflour
1½ tsp vanilla essence
2 tsp lemon juice
450 ml (¾ pint) double cream
110 g (4 oz) shelled almonds or hazelnuts, toasted and chopped
300 ml (½ pint) clotted cream
16 ripe passionfruit *

* If it's difficult to obtain fresh passionfruits, any sharp-flavoured soft fruit will suffice (e.g. pineapple, blueberries, raspberries, etc.).

Method

Preheat the oven to 140°C/275°F/Gas 1. Cut two baking parchment sheets to fit two smooth-surfaced baking trays.

Add the salt to the egg whites and whisk until peaks form, adding the sugar gradually as you whisk. When the mix is stiff, add the cornflour, vanilla essence and lemon juice, and divide into eight equal-sized portions. Spoon each portion into round nests on the trays about 4 cm (1½ in) thick, and bake for about 50–55 minutes, or until the outer shell of the Pavlova meringue is a pale champagne colour and has a solid feel. Remove from the oven and separate from the baking parchment.

When cold, spread a 1 cm (½ in) layer of double cream over each Pavlova, sprinkle with nuts and dot about with clotted cream. Finally, cut each passion-fruit in half and, using a small teaspoon, scoop out the pulp and spread the contents of two onto a single mini Pavlova.

STARTER 35

Bresaola, rocket and truffle cheese

Bresaola is essentially raw fillet of beef that has been cured in brine and air-dried, ready to be eaten within a couple of months. In principle it is similar to Parma ham, but the taste is more delicate and the texture a little more robust than any prosciutto. Traditionally from the valleys of Lombardy, it is served as a starter at serious dinners. Usually offered with some form of lemon, olive oil and black pepper dressing, we have adapted it to accompany a rocket salad and some shavings of truffle cheese. The cheese is infused with shavings of black truffles and has a pungent, crumbly texture – you don't need much of it.

Basically, curing the beef is a combination of 'corning' it (that is, salting it in brine) and marinating it in wine as you would for a pot-roast.

1.1 kg (2½ lb) beef sirloin, trimmed of all fat and sinew

Marinade
½ bottle white wine
½ bottle red wine
550 g (1¼ lb) sea salt
4 garlic cloves, peeled
1 cinnamon stick
6 whole cloves
12 black peppercorns
4 bay leaves
2 large sprigs fresh rosemary
2 large sprigs fresh thyme

To finish and serve
extra-virgin olive oil
truffle cheese *
120 g (4½ oz) rocket leaves

* Available from Patricia Michelson's splendid cheese shop in Islington, La Fromagerie. Tel: 0171 359 7440 for mail-order supplies.

Marinade method

Pour the wines into a large basin and stir in the salt until it is dissolved. Then add the garlic, spices and herbs. Place the beef in the liquid so that it is completely covered. Clingfilm the bowl and place in the fridge for one week. The brine will draw out most of the meat's excess moisture and this is then discarded.

Take out the beef and drain, then pat dry with a sterile kitchen cloth or tea towel. Wrap in a clean muslin cloth and hang in a cool well-ventilated place (such as a cold larder) for one week. This will dry out the outside of the joint and render the overall texture more dense and not unlike Parma ham.

After a week, rub the outside of the joint with some olive oil, which will prevent the outer skin hardening off further. The beef can then be sliced wafer-thin. Only serve the slices which are cut after an inch or so of 'end' has been removed, revealing the moister inner core of meat. The slices must be kept very thin as the meat is still quite chewy.

To serve

Dress the slices with shavings of truffle cheese and serve with a lightly dressed rocket salad. A good-quality extra-virgin olive oil is sufficient – a sharp dressing would compete too much with the other flavours.

MAIN COURSE 35

Roast goose with Nosh gourmet stuffing and potato and onion rösti with bilberries

Suggested accompaniments

Sugar-snap peas with ham and onions (see page 151)

Nosh gourmet stuffing
50 g (2 oz) slightly salted butter
1 medium onion, peeled and finely chopped
2 large cooking apples, peeled, cored and chopped
80 g (3 oz) prunes, stoned and coarsely chopped
1 garlic clove, peeled and crushed
25 g (1 oz) shelled hazelnuts, roughly chopped
25 g (1 oz) toasted almonds, roughly chopped
25 g (1 oz) pine nuts
2 slices granary or brown bread, crustless, finely crumbed
110 g (4 oz) cooked wild rice (see page 86)
80 g (3 oz) white grapes, seeded
juice of ½ orange
1 tbsp chopped fresh thyme

Goose
1 large goose, wild preferably (allow 675 g / 1½ lb for each person), drawn (i.e. gutted) weight *
2 wine glasses white wine
300 ml (½ pint) chicken stock (see page 155)
sea salt and freshly ground black pepper

* Goose must be under two years old. If one is being hung for you, find one with down on its legs and soft and 'pliable' feet and bill. Older birds will tend to be chewy or stringy.

Stuffing method

Heat the butter in a frying pan and cook the onion until soft and golden. Add the apple, prunes and garlic and fry for 1 minute. Then add the hazelnuts, almonds, and pine nuts and take the pan off the heat. Mix in the crumbs, wild rice and grapes. To this mixture add 1 tbsp of the stock, the orange juice and thyme. Season with salt and black pepper and stuff into the cavity of the bird.

Goose method

After stuffing, prick the skin all over with a fork through the fat layers on the back and around the tail, wings and legs. This helps fat drain out during cooking (it can be collected and potatoes roasted in it taste great). A wild bird will have less fat to drain out, so this pricking process is particularly important in a farmed bird.

Do not brush with oil. Place on a wire rack or trivet and roast until the thigh joint moves easily. The skin should be crisp. This will take about 15 minutes per 450 g (1 lb) approximately, but monitor the bird a few times towards the end to ensure it does not dry out. Average birds will take about 2–2½ hours. You will need to siphon off the fat every now and again,* as the amounts rendered are copious.

Remove the cooked bird to a warmed serving dish and cover with foil to keep it warm.* Pour out any remaining fat, leaving the tasty debris in the pan. Add the wine to the pan and deglaze the meat juices from the pan bottom, then transfer these juices to a saucepan. Skim off any excess fat with kitchen paper, add the remaining stock, and reduce the pan juices by a third. Test for seasoning** and then serve the gravy with the carved meat.

Any juice that runs out of the meat while it is resting can be poured back into the gravy for added flavour.

***Don't over-season at the beginning, otherwise you'll get a stock that is too salty 'on reduction'. Correct seasoning at the end.*

Potato and onion rösti with bilberries

Rösti are as typically Swiss as Gruyère and fondue. They vary from canton to canton, some using raw potatoes and some parboiled. They can include additional items such as cheese, bacon, herbs, caraway seeds, offal and even black coffee!

We have adapted here a version with onion that has travelled to central northern Germany where it is eaten as a side dish, traditionally with preserved, bottled bilberries (the potato pancakes being so rich that they require something rather acidic to accompany them).

Desirée is a variety of potato that gives good results, but almost any one that is not a waxy 'new' variety will be fine.

675 g (1½ lb) potatoes, peeled and finely grated
1 tsp fine table salt
1 Spanish onion, peeled and finely grated
1½ tsp sea salt
5 small eggs, lightly beaten
6 tbsp dry white breadcrumbs
freshly ground black pepper

oil for frying (sunflower, corn or peanut are good)
600 ml (1 pint) bottled bilberries (any sharp fruits like redcurrants or blueberries will be OK)

Method

Peel and finely grate the potato, then sprinkle with the salt. Mix and let the juices drain out (squeeze the potato against the side of a wire sieve). Discard the juices. Stir the finely grated onion, the sea salt and the eggs into the potato and mix together. It will be a little sloppy so add some breadcrumbs to soak up and stiffen the mix. Season with black pepper. Divide the mixture into rösti about 10 cm (4 in) in diameter and 1 cm (⅜ in) thick.

Heat some oil in a large heavy-based pan on a medium flame and shallow-fry the rösti, flattening each pancake with the back of a spoon, until crisp and brown on both sides. Try not to cook these too quickly or the centre of the rösti will be raw-tasting and crunchy. Try a couple for 3–4 minutes each side and adjust the time according to your stove heat. It is also important to have the oil at the right temperature: too hot, and the rösti will be raw inside and over-brown on the edges; too cool, and they will tend to absorb the oil and become soggy and inedible. Serve with the bilberries.

DESSERT 35

Rambutan and orange fruit salad

These fruits are very refreshing after a rich main course. Rambutans can be found in good supermarkets. They resemble a lychee with a spiny covering of bristles. They have a smooth shiny seed inside just like a lychee, which should be removed.

16 rambutans, peeled and seeded
8 oranges, peeled, cored and segmented
4 ripe peaches, skinned and thinly sliced
pulp of 8 passionfruits
3 tbsp Cointreau
1 tbsp fresh lime juice
a few sprigs of washed, fresh mint
14 kiwifruits, peeled and puréed

Method

Combine all the ingredients except for the kiwi purée in a glass bowl for half an hour before serving. Spoon the purée on to a dessert plate and, removing the mint, top with the fruit mixture.

STARTER 36

Sashimi of fresh ocean fish with a wasabi vinaigrette

The following selection is a suggestion only. Firm-fleshed fish tend to work best. The one important point to remember is that the fish must be as fresh as possible, and kept in the most hygienic of conditions.

110 g (4 oz) each of salmon fillet, yellowfin tuna
*   loin fillet, octopus, prawns, fatty tuna fillet*
*   and abalone*
150 ml (¼ pint) vinaigrette (see page 154)

1 tsp wasabi powder (Japanese 'horseradish')

Method

Trim and clean the fish well, removing bones, skin, membranes and discoloured parts. Wrap in clingfilm and place in the deep freeze for half an hour. This will 'harden' the flesh, firming it enough to allow for very thin slicing.

Arrange thin slices overlapping on the plate, and dress with the basic vinaigrette mixed with the wasabi powder.

MAIN COURSE 36

Char-grilled rib-eye steak with Chinese noodles, spring onions and shiitake mushrooms

8 × 225 g (8 oz) beef rib-eye steaks, bone
*   removed*
1 tbsp black bean sauce mixed with 2 tbsp
*   water*
4 tbsp olive oil
2 tbsp peanut oil
1 green pepper, skinned, cored and chopped
2 bunches spring onions, chopped
2 garlic cloves, peeled and finely chopped
1 × 1 cm (½ in) piece fresh ginger, peeled
700 g (1½ lb) fresh shiitake mushrooms,
*   sliced*
a few drops of sesame oil
700 g (1½ lb) Chinese egg noodles, blanched,
*   refreshed in cold water and well drained*

2 tbsp light soy sauce
3 tbsp chicken stock (see page 155)

Method

Season the steaks lightly with the black bean sauce and rest at room temperature for 30 minutes. Pre-heat a char-grill, overhead grill or grill pan.

Brush the steaks with the olive oil and grill for 3 minutes on each side.

Meanwhile, in a hot wok, heat the peanut oil until nearly smoking. Add the green pepper, spring onions, garlic, ginger, mushrooms and sesame oil, and stir-fry for a few minutes. Add the noodles. Stir the noodles around for a few minutes, ensuring they do not stick or burn, and then add the soy and stock and toss together. Serve the meat on a bed of noodles.

DESSERT 36

Raspberry, mascarpone and almond tart

The pastry used in this recipe has no wheat flour at all, which makes it unusual. Other soft fruits can be used very successfully instead of raspberries, e.g. blueberries. In our researches we have found that if you use strawberries, you should substitute ground hazelnuts for the ground almonds – they have a more complementary flavour.

You will need a 25 cm (10 in) springform tin.

1 tsp hazelnut oil
150 g (5 oz) salted butter, softened
110 g (4 oz) caster sugar
about 225 g (8 oz) ground almonds
2 tbsp crème de cassis*

500 g (18 oz) mascarpone cream cheese
900 g (2 lb) fresh raspberries (about 8 small
    punnets)
1 × 350 g (12 oz) jar seedless raspberry jelly
juice of 1 lemon

⋆ Use the best-quality cassis – you will only need a
few drops if you can get the top gear.

Method

Grease the springform tin with the hazelnut oil and
cut greaseproof or baking parchment to fit the sides
and bottom.

In a mixing bowl, beat together the butter and sugar
until creamy, and then add half the nuts: mix in
gently, then add the remainder by degrees. You want
to end up with a dough that does not feel sticky or
oily to the hands, so you may not need the entire
amount. Press a layer down on the bottom of the tin,
5 mm (¼ in) thick, and prick all over the surface
with a fork (to stop the pastry 'ballooning' when
baking).

Bake for about 15 minutes in a medium hot oven
(180–190°C/350–375°F/Gas 4–5). Check that the
pastry does not burn, but has coloured up slightly to
a golden-brown colour. Allow to cool completely.

Meanwhile, whisk the cassis into the mascarpone.
When the pastry has cooled, unclip the sides and
spread the mascarpone mix onto the surface, then
place the fruits tightly in a single layer to cover. Make
a glaze by boiling the jelly with the lemon juice for a
couple of minutes. Allow to cool for 15 minutes, then
brush over the fruits to glaze them.

Chill in the fridge for half an hour to set the glaze,
and then it is ready to serve. Remember when cutting
to allow for the disc of greaseproof paper underneath.

Blinis with smoked eel, soured cream and Beluga caviar

1 sachet easy-blend dried yeast
950 ml (1 pint 12 fl oz) warm (blood heat) milk
2 tsp melted unsalted butter
2 tsp caster sugar
4 eggs, separated
360 g (12½ oz) plain white flour
1 tsp sea salt
1 tbsp soured cream

  To cook and serve
sunflower oil for frying
110 g (4 oz) smoked eel, thinly sliced
150 ml (½ pint) thick soured cream⋆
50 g (2 oz) Beluga caviar

⋆ Soured cream is sometimes too runny for dolloping
on to hot blinis, so you can mix in some of the stiffer
crème fraiche (the French equivalent) to thicken the
mixture.

Method

Combine the yeast with the milk then with the
butter, sugar and egg yolks, and then stir this mixture
with a whisk until smooth. Add to the flour gradually, whisking in until no lumps remain. Add the salt
and set aside to rest.

Next whisk the egg whites until they form stiff peaks

and fold into the batter with the soured cream. Cover the bowl with clingfilm and allow to rise in a warm place for 30 minutes.

Spoon the batter into a frying pan and shallow-fry in hot oil over a medium heat until light brown on both sides. You need eight large blinis. Drain each blini on kitchen paper and keep warm until all are ready.

To serve, lay a couple of slices of smoked eel on each blini, spoon on some thick soured cream and dress with a couple of heaped teaspoonsful of Beluga caviar.

MAIN COURSE 37

Fillet of sea bass on samphire

8 × 150–175 g (5–6 oz) fillets of sea bass
    (16 × 110 g (4 oz) fillets will do) *
1 tbsp each of plain flour and fine ground polenta
    flour, mixed
sea salt and ground white pepper
6 tbsp olive oil
4 garlic cloves, peeled
juice of 1 lemon
4 spring onions, finely chopped
50 g (2 oz) fennel, blanched and finely chopped
2 medium carrots, peeled and finely chopped
1 thin leek, cleaned and finely chopped
120 ml (4 fl oz) dry champagne
675 g (1½ lb) fresh samphire, cleaned and
    trimmed of woody parts
25 g (1 oz) unsalted butter
2 tbsp finely chopped chervil
a squeeze of lemon

* *Due to changes in the coastal environment, wild sea bass have become rarer, and farmed sea bass are now available in most good supermarkets. Adjust your size of portion according to the fish available.*

Sea bass method

Clean the fillets, and trim clear of fins, spines, etc. Press each slice lightly into the flour mix, season and pan-fry in 2 tbsp of the oil on a high heat, with the garlic. A couple of minutes should be enough on each side. Lift the fillets out, squeeze lemon juice over them, and keep them warm on a roasting tray in a very low oven (140°C/275°F/Gas 1).

Meanwhile, sweat the vegetables in the same pan as you used for the fish, with the remaining oil, turning frequently to prevent browning. When soft, discard the garlic, add the champagne and simmer for 1 minute. The juices will thicken slightly.

Serve each fillet with a generous portion of vegetables and some sauce, on top of a bed of samphire, and sprinkled with chopped chervil.

Samphire method

Wash the samphire well, then blanch in boiling salted water for 30 seconds. Drain well, then simply stir-fry it briefly with butter. There is no need for additional strong spices in this recipe – just a squeeze of lemon.

DESSERT 37

Nosh caramelized apple pie with calvados cream

Pastry
350 g (12 oz) plain flour
200 g (7 oz) unsalted butter, softened
1 tsp caster sugar
a pinch of salt
1 large egg
1 tbsp cold milk

Pie
14 medium dessert apples
lemon juice
a pinch of powdered cinnamon
a small pinch of ground cloves
110 g (4 oz) butter
175 g (6 oz) caster sugar
60 ml (2 fl oz) calvados
500 ml (18 fl oz) fresh double cream
2 eggs

Pastry method

Put the flour on a surface or in a bowl, and make a well in the centre. Cut the butter into small pieces and put into the well along with the sugar, salt and egg. Rub all the ingredients together, pulling a little more of the flour in each time until all the ingredients have nearly come together. Add the milk, mix, then knead the dough a couple of times. Do not overwork the pastry. Place in a polythene bag and chill for 1 hour before use.

Pie method

Peel, halve and core all the apples. Leave eight halves whole for later,* and slice the remainder into a saucepan with 2 tbsp water and the spices.

* *The apple halves should be kept in water with the lemon juice to prevent discoloration.*

Gently simmer the apple slices until soft, then whisk them roughly with a fork. Set aside.

Grease a 25 cm (10 in) springform tin and roll out the pastry to a thickness of 3 mm (⅛ in). Drape it over the tin, releasing slack to get it to settle into the bottom edge. Do not stretch the pastry, otherwise it will collapse on baking and flop down into the centre. To avoid this happening, place a greaseproof paper circle on the pastry and fill with some baking beans to weigh it down. Bake blind in a preheated oven (220°C/425°F/Gas 7) for 15–20 minutes, then remove the beans and paper. Fill the bottom with the stewed apple and set aside in a warm place.

Reduce the oven temperature to 200°C/400°F/Gas 6. Next, in a heavy-based pan melt the butter, then add the sugar and stir until it melts. Now place the drained apple halves, round side down, in the sugar mix and turn up the heat to caramelize the sugar, at the same time as rolling them around to brown the peaks of the apples. When the apples are browned on both sides, place them on top of the stewed apple in the baking tin, round side up.

Continue to cook the caramel until it turns a rich dark brown (take care not to burn it, otherwise it will taste bitter). Pour in the calvados, and stir around to deglaze the caramel. Beat the double cream and eggs together, then add to the caramel. Pour over the apple layers and bake in the oven for 25 minutes. Leave the tart to set slightly, but serve warm.

Accompaniments

Accompaniments

Bobby beans with a warm lemon and caper vinaigrette

Fine Kenyan green beans look very chic on a plate but very often their taste is disappointing. Bobby beans are a good English alternative, as thick as a pencil and about 5 cm (6 in) long. They don't need stringing, and are rarely chewy. Here they are served warm with a vinaigrette, and they make a good salad on their own.

1.4 kg (3 lb) bobby beans (trimmed weight)
sea salt and freshly ground black pepper
juice of 2 lemons
150 ml (¼ pint) vinaigrette (see page 154)
2 garlic cloves, peeled and crushed
25 g (1 oz) pickled caper berries, drained

Method

Blanch the beans in boiling salted water for about 3–4 minutes. You want them to be firm and crunchy, but not with a raw uncooked taste. Meanwhile, squeeze the lemon juice into the vinaigrette, and stir in the garlic and capers.

When the beans are cooked al dente, drain and season them, then pour over the dressing while they are still warm. The heat of the vegetables will transfer to the dressing, and the flavours will develop well together.

Braised beans

This is delicious served with grilled rump of lamb (see page 69). Strain the marinade and add it with the stock.

400 g (14 oz) dried borlotti or lima beans*
110 g (4 oz) smoked streaky bacon, chopped
1 Spanish onion, peeled and chopped
2 garlic cloves, peeled and chopped
1 large carrot, chopped
2 celery stalks, peeled of the stringy bits and chopped
a small handful of chopped parsley
1 tsp chopped thyme
2 tbsp olive oil
1.4 litres (2½ pints) beef or veal stock (see page 155)
salt and freshly ground black pepper

* You can buy ready-cooked beans in cans from supermarkets. Simply drain and rinse, then cook as above, but using your common sense to reduce the amount of added liquid and the simmering time accordingly.

Method

Pour boiling water over the beans and leave to soak overnight. In the morning, drain and rinse. Sauté the bacon, onion, garlic, carrot, celery and herbs gently in the oil until soft and golden. Add the beans, cover with the stock, and simmer, covered, until the beans are tender (about 2–2½ hours depending on the size and age of the beans).

Remove half the beans and mash them, then return them to the bean pan and season.

Caramelized carrots

1.8 kg (4 lb) best-quality carrots, peeled
600 ml (1 pint) light chicken stock (see
*   page 155)*
80 g (3 oz) unsalted butter
2 heaped tsp fine soft brown sugar
finely chopped parsley

Method

Cut the carrots into medium large chunks, and place in a large saucepan. Pour in enough light chicken stock to just cover them. Bring to the boil and reduce the heat slightly to keep a medium fast boil until the liquid reduces to almost dry. This will take about 20 minutes. The vegetables will be quite soft at this stage.

Then swirl the butter around the pan with the sugar. Turn up the flame to high, and the sugar will start to caramelize and coat the carrots. Turn the flame down to medium after a couple of minutes and turn the vegetables evenly so the sugar does not catch and burn. When the carrots have an even coating of sticky brown mix, they are done. Simply serve with fresh chopped parsley.

Celeriac and carrot purée

You will need a fine mesh mouli for this.

2 heads of celeriac
1.4 kg (3 lb) sweet carrots
chicken stock to cover (see page 155)
50 g (2 oz) unsalted butter
sea salt and freshly ground black pepper

Peel the celeriac thickly to remove any brown spots, and cut into small dice. Peel the carrots, and cut them into slightly larger dice.*

* *The celeriac is somewhat more woody than the carrot, so cut the latter larger so that they will arrive at the same 'softness point' together.*

Cover the veg dice with chicken stock and bring to the boil. Simmer for about 20 minutes (if you don't cook it enough, the mouli will clog and jam with stringy bits of celeriac). Drain* when soft, add the butter and pass through the fine mesh of a mouli. Season and mix together. This purée can be made in advance and reheated gently on a low flame, so long as it's stirred constantly. This also tends to reduce any extra moisture in the purée.

* *The drained root vegetable liquid can make an interesting base for a minestrone-type soup at a later date – it can be frozen for future use.*

Chilli sherry

This culinary secret was shown to Mick by some local Maltese chefs as a good way of livening up fish soups. It's also become a Nosh tradition for sharpening up Bloody Marys.

Into a sterilized white wine (clear glass) bottle place 4 large whole fresh red chillies (previously blanched for 15 seconds in boiling water). Pour over them a bottle of dry sherry. Use something like a fino; cream or medium sherries do not seem to work well with this idea. Leave to steep for about three weeks and you can pour a few drops into risottos, gravies, soups and many sauces.

Creamed beetroot

This makes a great-tasting accompaniment. Perfect with all beef dishes. Coarsely grate cooked whole beetroots into a béchamel sauce made with single cream instead of milk – enough sauce to coat the beetroot. Add a dash of lemon juice and plenty of freshly ground black pepper and stir slowly in a saucepan to reheat.

Dauphinoise potatoes

This is a rich dish by nature, and you should not engage in any misguided attempt to reduce the rich ingredients or you will not get the proper results. Any of that nonsense and you're in trouble.

2.25 kg (5 lb) potatoes (Desirée or Maris Piper are good)
3 garlic cloves, peeled and crushed
40 g (1½ oz) butter, softened
2 medium onions, peeled and finely sliced
sea salt and freshly ground black pepper
1 tsp freshly grated nutmeg
225 g (8 oz) Gruyère or Raclette cheese, grated
450 ml (¾ pint) single cream
110 g (4 oz) Parmesan, finely grated
4 tbsp extra-virgin olive oil

Method

Parboil the potatoes in their skins until waxy, but not falling apart, and then when cool enough skin them and slice into 5 mm (¼ in) thick slices. Meanwhile, rub and squeeze one of the crushed garlic cloves around an earthenware dish (one with an edge about 5 cm/2 in high is best). Then rub softened butter all over the base and sides to minimize sticking.

Place some of the onion rings over the base of the dish, and build up a layer of potato slices over this, laying the potatoes against each other. (This will create space between to help the cream penetrate to the middle of the dish.) Season with salt, black pepper and nutmeg, and sprinkle with Gruyère or Raclette cheese. Then add another layer of potato, arranged so the slices go the other way. Again, this

will help the cream to get into the dish. Season as before, adding a few onion rings for flavour. Then add cheese on top and start the final layer of potato.

When the top layer is finished, pour over the single cream, season, add the rest of the Gruyère and then the grated Parmesan using the olive oil for extra richness.

Bake in a hot oven (220°C/425°F/Gas 7) for about 20–25 minutes or until the top is golden brown.

Fennel

Trim and slice a large bulb into 5 mm (¼ in) thick slices (removing the v-shaped thick 'root' at the base of the bulb. Pan-fry quickly and then bake in an oven preheated to 200°C/400°F/Gas 6 in its own pan for at least 5–7 minutes, but with a little chicken stock (see page 155) in the bottom of the dish to keep it moist.

Foccaccia with black olives and herbs

Foccaccia is one of our favourite types of bread. Recipes differ but we have never tasted better than the *pane Milanese* with black olives made by Dan Schickentanz of de Gustibus. He is a master baker in the true sense of the word and the recipe below is just a sample of his craft. Apologies for stealing it, Dan, but it was your turn! You will need two large mixing bowls (preferably non-metallic), a 25 cm (10 in) springform tin, a pastry brush, a tea towel and clingfilm.

500 g (18 oz) strong white bread flour

300 ml (½ pint) tepid spring water

1 sachet dried easy-blend yeast

50 ml (2 fl oz) olive oil

1 tbsp sea salt

1 tbsp dried Italian herbs (oregano, thyme, basil,
   sage, parsley, etc,)

200 g (7 oz) whole black olives – pit them
   yourself to give about 150 g (5 oz)

50 g (2 oz) pumpkin seeds

Method

Put half the flour into one large bowl with all the water, and mix. Cover with the tea towel and leave at room temperature overnight (at least 12 hours).

In the other bowl mix the remainder of the flour with the yeast and the rested overnight flour/water mix, and stir until well combined. Next, mix in half the olive oil and then knead the dough on a lightly floured surface. Add a little more flour or water to adjust the texture of the dough: it should have a slack kind of feel. (When formed into a ball it should not stay in a ball but rather spread out slightly.) *Do not* add too much flour.

Mix by hand, about 15 minutes, or in a mixer if you are lazy like us, for 10 minutes. In the last 5 minutes add the salt. Make into a ball, place in a greased plastic bag and blow it up. Twist the top into a knot to seal it, and let it prove in a warm, not hot, place for 1 hour until it has doubled in size. (Alternatively a clingfilmed bowl will do.)

Mix the rest of the oil, the herbs and the pitted olives in a blender, or hand-chop finely.

Take the inflated risen dough and punch it down. Form it into a ball again, and let it rest for another 15 minutes.

Place the dough on a floured board and make into a disc twice the diameter of the springform tin. Spread half the olive mix in the middle and fold the outside edges of the dough to the centre, slightly overlapping. Now the size should be slightly smaller than the tin size. Place it upside down into the greased tin and press with your fingertips hard all over the surface to make a dimpled surface. You should end up with the filling breaking through in a few places. Now take the rest of the olive mix and spread it on top of the dough. Sprinkle the pumpkin seeds on next and repeat the prodding routine. Put the covered tin (the plastic bag routine works well again) in a warm place, and leave for about 1 hour to double in size once more. Don't knock or bang the tin or surface though, as it may deflate the dough and will ruin your efforts.

Halfway through your waiting time, preheat the oven to 220°C/425°F/Gas 7. Place the tin in the oven and reduce the temperature immediately to 170°C/340°F/Gas 3–4 for 25–30 minutes. You can cover the top of the bread with foil to prevent any edges burning if required. Let cool for 3 hours before cutting.

It seems like a lot of work, but we guarantee it will be delicious and worth your while.

Garlic mashed potato

1.8 kg (4 lb) old floury potatoes

sea salt and ground white pepper

3 bulbs garlic, whole and unpeeled

12 tbsp extra-virgin olive oil

Method

While the spuds are boiling roast the garlic bulbs in a hot oven (200°C/400°F/Gas 6) for 15–20 minutes. When cool enough to touch, squeeze out the white creamy pulp into the olive oil. Whisk the roast garlic and oil into the mash and season well.

Lyonnaise-style sauté potatoes

1.4 kg (3 lb) Desirée potatoes
6 tbsp olive oil
2 tbsp unsalted butter
a handful of fresh parsley, chopped
sea salt and freshly ground black pepper

Method

Peel and cut the potatoes into 1 cm (½ in) dice and parboil for 10 minutes, draining them dry very thoroughly.

Heat the oil over a medium flame, add the butter, and fry the potatoes until a golden-brown colour. Drain and put in a hot dish. Stir in the chopped parsley, salt and pepper throughout.

Mashed potato

For best results with mashed potato, firstly choose the varieties listed on the supermarket bags and label tags as being best for this particular type of cooking. Boil the spuds in plenty of well salted water. Use a coarse-mesh mouli to get the mash sieved well with no lumps, but with a good even texture. Add good-quality butter and cream or even virgin olive oil for a different flavour. Don't be frightened to add some sea salt (Maldon is good) and a pinch of white pepper, or even freshly grated nutmeg. So many people today are paranoid about salting foods. Don't be frightened, but be sparing – don't kill the flavours. But remember, trust your taste buds, they're there for a reason – for you to make up your own mind.

Mashed potato with soured cream and spring onions

For this particular accompaniment, add fresh soured cream as well as unsalted butter to the cooked mashed potato and whip well in with a whisk. The potato has a great ability to absorb the cream and butter, and will eventually achieve a smooth consistency. Place the potato in a well-buttered ovenproof dish and sprinkle the top liberally with chopped spring onion. Place under a hot grill for about 2 minutes to crisp up the top.

Mashed potato with chives

1.4 kg (3 lb) potatoes, peeled
sea salt and ground white pepper
150 ml (¼ pint) single cream
110 g (4 oz) unsalted butter, melted
1 large bunch fresh chives, chopped
a pinch of freshly grated nutmeg

Method

Add the cream and half the butter to the cooked mashed potato and mix in well. Meanwhile, steep the chopped chives in the remaining melted butter for 5 minutes. Swirl around occasionally. Season, add the nutmeg and mix well together.

Matchstick potatoes with anchovies and cream

These potatoes are great with roast gammon (see page 63). Take out the gammon to rest when you turn up the heat.

1.8 kg (4 lb) potatoes (Desirée are good)
50 g (2 oz) unsalted butter
sea salt and freshly ground black pepper

3 small cans anchovies, drained
900 ml (1½ pints) single cream
Parmesan (optional)

Method

Parboil the potatoes without peeling. When cool enough to touch, discard the skin and cut the potatoes – they should still be 'waxy' – into fine matchstick lengths. Grease a roasting tray with some of the butter and spread the matchsticks in a layer evenly, seasoning them as you spread them out and inserting the drained anchovies at intervals. Pour the cream evenly over the top and dot with butter or Parmesan. Bake at 180–190°C/350–375°F/Gas 4–5 on the top shelf of the oven for 20–25 minutes then turn the heat up to 200°C/400°F/Gas 6, and bake for a further 20 minutes. Allow to cool slightly for easy cutting into sections

Moon-dried tomatoes

We call these 'moon-dried tomatoes' in deference to the outdoor sun-dried Italian imports. You can make these easily in your own home while you sleep – literally! It is the Nosh Brothers' way to 'do-what-the-Italians-do-during-the-day-but-at-night' . . . if you know what we mean.

You must have the plum type of Italian tomatoes. It doesn't matter if they are a bit overripe or bruised. In fact, this recipe is perfect for tomatoes that are a bit squashy or 'over' for fresh salads.

Method

Wash the tomatoes and dry them. Next, cut them horizontally along the long centre line of the tomato (bisecting it from stem to point north to south). If the stem end has a very white hard pith core at the stalk point, remove that shaped bit with a sharp paring knife and discard it. Arrange the halves of the tomatoes, cut side up, on a wire cake rack on a flat baking tray. (It is important not to put them straight on to the baking tray as they will tend to burn on the bottom surface.)

Brush each cut surface with olive oil and season with sea salt and a twist of freshly ground black pepper. Bake in a very, very low oven (50°C/125°F/ the lowest possible gas) overnight until they have dried out and shrivelled somewhat. In Italy the tradition is to remove the seeds and core which gives a dryish, chewy result; with the watery core left in, there is a moister feel on the palate.

This is a dish that can be made after you have baked something in the oven on a high heat. All you have to do is to switch off the oven, place the racks of tomatoes inside and shut the door. The natural decrease in temperature will accommodate the process needed for best results. If you have an Aga solid-top-type oven, the plate-warming cupboard section is best for this. You may need to keep the tomatoes in for 24 hours even! Keep an eye on them. Slow and even is the way.

When the tomatoes have finished their drying-out process, they can be preserved in a Kilner jar of good-quality olive oil. The oil itself can even be flavoured with garlic and various herbs, such as thyme, to vary the results. So long as the dried tomatoes are covered with oil they will not become mildewed. They will keep for a couple of months in a cold place and about six in a fridge. The oil will then solidify so thaw it out if you just want to remove a couple of tomatoes for a single dish.

Purée of carrots with cumin butter

1.8 kg (4 lb) carrots, peeled and finely
chopped
1.2 litres (2 pints) chicken stock (see page 155)
50 g (2 oz) salted butter
2 tbsp single cream
1 tsp ground cumin
sea salt and freshly ground black pepper

Method

Place the carrots in a large saucepan with the chicken stock (to cover the carrots by 2.5 cm / 1 in), and bring to the boil. Cover with the lid and simmer on a very low heat for about 20 minutes until the core of each segment is quite soft. Then drain thoroughly and pass through the coarse mesh of a vegetable mouli. Add the butter, cream and cumin to the carrot purée. This mixture can either be served immediately while hot or can be reheated later when required. If reheating, remember to keep the flame low and stir frequently to prevent the mixture catching and sticking.

To serve, scoop neat tablespoon-sized dollops to the side of the dish.

Ratatouille

An excellent recipe stolen from Dilly Godfrey-Wild.

350 g (12 oz) aubergine, sliced into thumb-sized
batons
2 yellow peppers, seeded and cored
1 green pepper, seeded and cored
2 red peppers, seeded and cored
12 button onions, peeled, blanched and halved
500 g (18 oz) small green courgettes, sliced into
thumb-sized batons
1 kg (2¼ lb) plum tomatoes, skinned, seeded and
chopped

6 spring onions, sliced
8 tbsp olive oil
5 garlic cloves, peeled and chopped
1 large sprig fresh rosemary
4 bay leaves
a handful of flat-leafed parsley, chopped

Method

Cook all the vegetables separately in a little of the oil. First fry the garlic lightly over a medium heat, then add the rosemary. Now cook the vegetables in the flavoured oil. Set each vegetable aside as cooked, draining each time, leaving the aubergine until last. Add dashes of olive oil as needed throughout the cooking process. Next combine all the vegetables in the pan, slot in the bay leaves, and cook gently, covered, for about 15 minutes until tender. Stir parsley throughout.

Roast potatoes

2.25 kg (5 lb) old potatoes
sea salt and freshly ground black pepper
3 tbsp goose fat or beef dripping

Method

Some people cook their potatoes from raw, and some parboil them. If parboiled, they cook quicker, and being floury in texture they absorb more of the roasting fat and get a better, crisper result.

Boil the potatoes whole in their skins for about 10 minutes, depending on their size, and refresh in cold water. Skin them and slice partly down one side, in 5 mm (¼ in) 'slots', like a comb. This has the effect of giving a larger surface area for the heat to penetrate and the flavours to be absorbed. The potatoes should then be sprinkled liberally with sea salt and black pepper. Heat the goose fat or beef dripping until smoking hot in a roasting tray and then pile the spuds into the tray, taking care not to splash the fat around. Place in the oven towards the latter half of the meat cooking time until they are brown and crisp. You should check them halfway so that any well-done outside edges are rearranged to ensure even cooking.

Sauté potatoes

This can be done with either old or new potatoes.

2.25 kg (5 lb) potatoes, peeled
2 tbsp goose fat
1 tbsp unsalted butter
sea salt and freshly ground black pepper

Method

Whether you like the waxy or floury type of potato, the method remains the same: parboil the potatoes, cut into convenient 1 cm (½ in) chunks, and fry in the hot fat and butter over a high flame until golden-brown and crisp.

Savoy cabbage

Savoy cabbage has a robust texture and flavour, and is much underrated. However, the addition of just a little garlic is perfect. Follow this method and your memories of nightmare school dinners will be exorcized for ever.

1 garlic clove, peeled and crushed
50 g (2 oz) unsalted butter
1 large Savoy cabbage
300 ml (½ pint) hot light chicken stock (see page 155)
a large pinch of freshly grated nutmeg
salt and ground white pepper

Method

Trim off any yellowed or torn bits from the cabbage but try to retain as many as possible of the outer leaves, as the dark green parts have much of the strong flavour needed here. Slice the cabbage in two, remove the tough stalk at the base and slice the leaves into 1 cm (½ in) wide strips across the grain of the layers.

Sauté the garlic in the butter for a couple of minutes on a low heat without letting it brown, and then add the cabbage, turning it regularly for another 3–4 minutes. Then add half the hot stock and the nutmeg, put a lid on the pot, and braise for another 5 minutes or so, turning occasionally. Like pasta, the cabbage should be slightly 'al dente' with a moist coating of the reduced juices. Check the texture by chewing a strand in the same way, remembering that the cabbage will continue to cook on in a heavy-based pot. If needed, add more stock to the cabbage, but don't drown it – the residue should just cover and cling to the cabbage, the butter giving it a good shine. If necessary, season only lightly – the stock should have seasoned it enough.

Sugar-snap peas and Jersey Royals

Dead easy accompaniment, this. Just remember that sugar-snap peas need only a 30-second blanching in boiling water before tossing in butter with sea salt and freshly ground black pepper in a hot wok. They should have a crisp bite to their texture. Consequently, don't prepare them until the last minute. If they are made too far ahead of time they'll get wrinkly and insipid and lose that 'bite'.

Jersey Royals are around for all too short a time. Just scrub them lightly, keeping that tasty feathery skin on and don't overcook them. Five minutes of boiling time is plenty for the small ones. Best served with Jersey butter and plenty of chopped chives.

Sugar-snap peas with ham and onions

16 spring onions
8 garlic cloves
450 g (1 lb) sugar-snap peas, trimmed
450 g (1 lb) mangetouts, trimmed
4 slices honey-roast ham
2 tbsp single cream

Method

Blanch the spring onions and garlic cloves in boiling salted water for 1 minute. Remove the garlic skins. Finely chop both. Plunge the sugar-snap peas into the fast-boiling salted water for 30 seconds, then add the mangetouts for another 30 seconds. Drain and set aside.

In a large frying pan, sauté the ham, spring onions and garlic for 2 minutes in the oil. Add the cream and the peas and mangetout and toss the mix thoroughly. Transfer to a warmed dish for serving.

Sweet and sour red cabbage

1 large red cabbage
2 eating apples, peeled, cored and chopped
50 g (2 oz) raisins
250 ml (8 fl oz) wine vinegar
110 g (4 oz) soft brown sugar
sea salt and freshly ground black pepper
50 g (2 oz) unsalted butter

Method

Slice the cabbage thinly and place in a deep casserole dish with a lid, with the apple, raisins, wine vinegar, sugar and seasonings. Bring to the boil, and stir the mixture, ensuring the sugar does not burn at the bottom. Cover with the lid, reduce the heat and simmer for at least 45 minutes. Check that it does not dry out, and add small dashes of water as necessary.

Towards the end, add the butter to give it a shine and turn the mixture, adjusting seasoning to taste if necessary.

Vanilla sugar

Vanilla pods are quite expensive to buy in the UK, but their delicate flavour can be made good use of by splitting a couple of pods down one side and placing them in a jam jar with a screw-top lid, then filling up to near the top with caster sugar. The vanilla oils will permeate the sugar in a couple of days and within the week the flavour and aroma will be quite strong. Use to sprinkle on top of puddings and to flavour custards and ice creams.

Dressings

Home-made vinegar

Vinegars are basically grape wines changed from a sweet nature to a sour one by friendly bacteria and fermentation, not dissimilar to the way milk is turned into yogurt. You will need one large dark glass bottle (brewing jar or old magnum-sized wine bottle).

1 tbsp vinegar liquor ('mother culture')
150–300 ml (¼–½ pint) old left-over red wine*

* *Don't be tempted to use the remnants in guests' wine glasses. Wine that has contacted a person's mouth may contaminate the mother and ruin the whole brew, so only use wine left over in the bottles.*

Method

The mother culture, when viewed in the bottom of a glass bottle, can appear as a grey slime, or sometimes, when more established, as dark leafy layers, like old tea leaves. The culture needs some warmth to get started and you should place it in a sterile container (Milton liquid is a good sterilizer) with a narrow neck and pour on some wine to get it started. Too much wine in one go will literally kill the culture with the alcohol, so you should start it off gradually, with a glass or two, and then add more after a week or so. The process should take about three weeks at room temperature to go from wine to final vinegar. When the liquid level is near the top you can decant three-quarters or so of it carefully, and keep it sealed in the normal way. It's useful to just keep pouring in the wine lees left in the last inch or so of wine bottles after dinner parties, and keeping the mother culture topped up.

If in doubt as to how your brew is progressing, just pour a slug into a shot glass and take a sniff and a sip! The better the grade of wine, the better the depth of flavour your vinegar will have, but even with inexpensive plonk, the results of using your own culture will be worth it.

In Europe, where these gourmet traditions are highly valued, 'mother cultures' have been handed down from generation to generation and are closely guarded secrets.

Once your mother is firmly established you can divide it into two by decanting off the existing vinegar, pouring half the slime culture into another sterile container and donating it to another gourmet friend who will be fascinated to grow his or her own vinegar.

Cultures may be purchased from specialist home-brewing shops.

Lemon-infused olive oil

You can buy lemon-infused olive oil ready for pouring but it's easily made at home.

Into a sterile clear glass bottle (an old empty olive oil bottle is fine), push wedges of fresh lemons that have been blanched in boiling water for a few minutes. This enables the waxy coating to be cleaned off with a dry cloth and ensures a sterile outer skin. (So long as you can keep the lemon slices immersed in the oil, they will not get furry with mildew.) Cap the bottle with a stainless-steel and cork drinks pourer and you will have a lemon oil for dressing fish or other foods within a week. The best oil to use is a medium-weight olive oil; this has a smooth, even light flavour. Some of the greeny, virgin first pressings are too strong and peppery in flavour and will mask the delicacy of any fish. The taste can be accentuated by also steeping peeled inner stems of lemongrass in the oil. This gives the oil an oriental taste.

Mayonnaise

3 small fresh egg yolks *
1 tbsp white wine vinegar
sea salt
1 tsp good-quality Dijon mustard
150 ml (¼ pint) good-quality olive oil
300 ml (½ pint) good-quality salad oil
*   (sunflower etc., but not soya)*
1 tsp lemon juice
a pinch of caster sugar

* *To remove the worries and fears about any lurking salmonella in raw egg, simply mix the yolks with the vinegar at the start and leave for 5–10 minutes, stirring once or twice. Salmonella hate vinegar and it will reduce the risk of any contamination.*

Method

Whisk the yolks and vinegar with some salt and the

mustard, then drizzle in the mixed oils, incorporating them thoroughly, beating all the time, until half the oil is used. Then add the lemon juice and continue to pour and whisk oil in. Finally, adjust the seasoning.

If the resulting mayo either looks too thin or has split or curdled, it is possible to rescue it by beating another yolk in a separate bowl and pouring the original mixture in gradually, beating well as before, but really taking plenty of time to whisk well together.

Walnut dressing

Make a walnut dressing with red wine vinegar, and a walnut and olive oil mix (1 part vinegar to 5 parts oil). As walnut oil is quite strong, mix it with olive oil 50:50. Add a pinch of sea salt, some freshly ground black pepper, a pinch of caster sugar, a small dab of grainy mustard (Meaux Pommery is good) and a few well-crushed shelled walnuts. Remember, seasonings do not dissolve in oil, so add everything first to the vinegar, and then whisk in the oil. (The sugar is there to balance the bitterness of the walnuts . . . it should not taste sweet as such.)

Vinaigrette

Use a basic mix of 1 part wine or cider vinegar to 3 parts virgin olive oil. Add salt and black pepper. Remember, salt does not dissolve in oil and should be added to the vinegar first. Whisk all the ingredients together. If liked, you can substitute lemon juice for half of the vinegar. Home-made vinegar is usually good to make (see page 152).

Stocks

The following stock recipes are intended to result in a moderately robust taste. Further intensity may be obtained by reduction by up to 50% for a 'rich' soup base and even 85% for a thick meat glaze. We've used the term 'light' with stocks to mean the unreduced types shown below.

Fish stock

You can buy fish stock cubes these days which, although OK, will not give as good a result as making your own. Fortunately, fish stock does not take long to make and doesn't need hours of brewing and simmering. If you can chat up your fishman, he'll probably give you the ingredients for free!

You can make this stock up to three days beforehand and keep it chilled in the fridge or keep it frozen for three months. Warm before using.

2.25 kg (5 lb) mixed fish bones, salmon heads, etc.
1 large Spanish onion, peeled and sliced
4 carrots
1 fennel bulb with feathery tops
1.75 litres (3 pints) water
4 black peppercorns
1 bottle light white wine
220 g (8 oz) mushrooms (stalks and peelings are OK)
1 bouquet garni (bay, parsley stalks, chervil)

Method

Just about any fish is suitable for stock, so long as you don't use really oily fish (mackerel, tuna, etc.). Salmon heads are usually in plentiful supply at any time of year, and flatfish give good flavours, having proportionately more skeleton than flesh. The only advice here is to ensure you remove any gills with stout scissors, as these sometimes give a bitter flavour to the stock – fiddly, but worth the effort!

Put all the ingredients into a large saucepan and bring to the boil. Skim off any scum or froth and discard it. Lower the heat to a slow simmer and cook the bones for about 45 minutes, continuing to skim as necessary. Longer than this isn't really needed, unlike meat stocks. You should then pass the liquid through a fine metal sieve or muslin to strain it. Discard the bones, etc. Then return the liquid to the saucepan and reduce it by at least one-quarter on a fast boil, so you end up with at least 1.75 litres (3 pints) well-flavoured stock.

Beef or Veal stock

For a veal stock, reverse the quantities of bones.

1.1 kg (2½ lb) broken beef bones and trimmings
450 g (1 lb) veal bones and trimmings
50 g (2 oz) streaky bacon, chopped
1 tbsp tomato purée
110 g (4 oz) carrots, finely diced
110 g (4 oz) mushrooms, finely diced
110 g (4 oz) onion, peeled and finely diced
110 g (4 oz) leek, finely diced
2 fresh tomatoes, de-seeded and skinned
1 shallot, peeled and chopped
2 garlic cloves, peeled and crushed
600 ml (1 pint) white wine
2.3 litres (4 pints) cold water
a bunch of parsley stalks
a pinch each of dried tarragon and chervil
1 bouquet garni (thyme, parsley, bay, etc.)
6 black peppercorns
1 clove

Method

Brown the beef and veal bones and trimmings in a hot oven (220°C/425°F/Gas 7) for 15–20 minutes, then place in a large stockpot with all the ingredients down to and including the white wine and bring to the boil. Boil until the wine has nearly evaporated and then add the cold water. Add the herbs, bouquet garni and spices, and bring to the boil. Simmer for 4 hours, skimming the surface frequently with a ladle to remove any scummy froth. When cooked, strain through a fine conical strainer. Now transfer the stock to a clean saucepan and place on a high heat to boil and reduce the stock by at least half its volume to render it strong tasting. You should end up with at least 1.4 litres (2½ pints) well-flavoured liquid. Resting the liquid in the fridge for a couple of hours when cooled ensures that any fat congeals on the top and can be removed easily.

Chicken stock

Make as per the above beef stock recipe substituting chicken (or even duck) bones for the veal bones (omitting the tomato purée) and adding 1 leek, 2 cloves and 450g (1lb) of chicken wings to intensify the chicken flavour. Giblets, when supplied with carcasses, are very useful as an addition too. (Although Mick can never resist the temptation to sauté them for a quick scoff!)

Index

(A)   denotes Accompaniments
(D)   denotes Dessert
(M)   denotes Main course
(S)   denotes Starter

almond, mascarpone and raspberry tart (D), 137
Amaretti rum truffle cake (D), 111
American breakfast cake (D), 63
apple
     baked (D), 115
     layer pudding (D), 76
     pie, caramelized (D), 140
     strudel (D), 24
     tart (D), 21
apricot and pecan cookies (D), 97
Armagnac and prune tart (D), 73
artichokes (S), 60
asparagus with Parmesan (S), 101

banana toffee pie (D), 87
beans
     bobby beans (A), 142
          with gammon, 62
     braised (A), 142
          with lamb, 69
     Tuscan soup (S), 91
beef
     bavette of (M), 47
     braised (M), 33
     Bresaola (S), 132
     calves' liver Veneziana (M), 102
     fillet parcels (M), 128
     fillet steak (M), 124
     pot roast (M), 71

beef (*continued*)
     rib-eye steak (M), 135
     roast (M), 113
beetroot, creamed (A), 143
     with beef, 113
black pudding, salad (S), 25
bread and butter pudding (D), 35
brill, pan fried (M), 23
bruschetta (S), 68

Camembert, Pont-L'Évêque and mustard fruits (D), 126
capellini with wild mushrooms (S), 88
carrots
     caramelized (A), 143
          with beef, 128
     purée of (A), 150
          with partridge, 108
          with pheasant, 119
celeriac and carrot purée (A), 143
champagne cocktail, 14
chicken
     breasts (M), 26
     satay (M), 66
     smoked, salad (S), 46
     Soto ayam Madura (S), 120
     Southern (M), 95
     stock (A), 155
     Valdostana (M), 90
chicory salad (S), 85
chilli sherry (A), 143
chocolate
     mousse (D), 51
     pie, hot (D), 99, 101
crab cakes (S), 56

crème brûlée (D), 69
crème caramel (D), 48
crostini (S), 43

date tart (D), 84
duck
    confit (M), 83
    liver *confit* (S), 98
    roast breast (M), 80
    pan fried with rocket salad (S), 70

eel, smoked (S), 138

fennel (A), 144
    with brill 23
feta cheese, Greek salad of (S), 49
fettucine with tomato and basil sauce
        (S), 32
figs in spiced vanilla syrup (D), 129
fish
    sashimi of (S), 135
    soup (S), 62
    stock (A), 154
foccaccia (A), 144
    with bean soup, 91
foie gras
    goose liver terrine (S), 127
    pan fried (S), 124

gammon, roast glazed spiced (M), 62
gazpacho (S), 83
goose, roast (M), 133
Gorgonzola, chicory and walnut salad, 85
guava cheesecake (D), 123

jackfruit fritters (D), 67

laksa, Singapore (S), 65
lamb
    grilled rump of (M), 69
    roast leg of (M), 92

langoustine ravioli (S), 129
leek and Roquefort tart (S), 29
lemon
    mousse (D), 28
    olive oil (A), 153
    pancakes (S), 31
    tart (D), 59
linguine
    with pork (M), 77
    with prawns (S), 115
lobster, grilled (M), 116

mascarpone, raspberry and almond tart (D),
        137
mayonnaise (A), 153
meringues (D), 131
monkfish
    brochettes of (M), 99
    ceviche of (S), 74
mushroom
    salad (S), 25, 79
    soup (S), 119
mussels (M), 41

olive oil, lemon infused (A), 153
orange and rambutan fruit salad (D), 134
osso bucco (M), 58
ostrich medallions, roast (M), 130

partridge, roast breasts of (M), 108
peaches in dessert wine (D), 46
pear(s)
    poached (D), 120
    tarte Tatin (D), 39
peas, sugar-snap, and Jersey Royals (A), 151
    with salmon, 61
peas, sugar-snap, with ham and onions (A), 152
    with goose, 133
pecan
    and apricot cookies (D), 97
    and raspberry *zuppa inglese* (D), 103

peppers
    roasted (S), 43
    spiced (S), 95
pheasant, roast breasts of (M), 119
Pont-L'Évêque, Camembert and mustard fruits
    (D), 126
pork
    Milanese (M), 77
    roast belly of (M), 50
    roast fillet of (M), 38
    roast suckling pig (M), 122
potatoes
    Dauphinoise (A), 144
        with pork, 38
    garlic mashed (A), 146
        with lamb, 69
    Lyonnaise-style (A), 146
        with partridge, 108
    mashed (A), 147
        with beef, 33
        with duck *confit*, 83
        with beef, 71
        with chicken, 26
    matchstick (A), 147
        with gammon, 62
    roast (A), 150
    sauté (A), 151
prune and Armagnac tart (D), 73

rambutan and orange fruit salad (D), 134
raspberry
    ice cream (D), 94
    mascarpone and almond tart (D), 137
    and pecan *zuppa inglese* (D), 103
ratatouille (A), 150
    with chicken, 90
red cabbage, sweet and sour (A), 152
    with pork, 38
red snapper, grilled (M), 75
rocket salad with pan-fried duck (S), 70
Roquefort and leek tart (S), 29

rujak (D), 82
rum cake (D), 118

salmon
    marinated fillets (M), 61
    in spinach leaf parcels (M), 85
sausages with sauerkraut (M), 30
Savoy cabbage (A), 151
    with beef, 33
scallops
    queen (S), 112
    king (S), 108
sea bass, pan fried (M), 139
Spaghetti carbonara Romana (M), 20
spinach
    con salsiccia (S), 20
    with smoked lardons (S), 37
squid
    with bruschetta (S), 68
    risotto of (M), 44
stocks (A), 154
stracciatella Romana (S), 76
strawberry(ies)
    dipped in chocolate (D), 78
    ice cream (D), 42
    with lemon juice and black pepper (D), 61

tiramisu (D), 90
tomatoes, moon-dried (A), 148
tortilla (S), 22

vanilla sugar (A), 152
veal stock (A), 155
vichyssoise (S), 40
vinaigrette (A), 154
vinegar, home-made (A), 152

walnut dressing (A), 154